MAVERICK STARTUP

11 X-FACTORS TO BOOTSTRAP FROM ZERO TO SIX FIGURES AND BEYOND

YANIK SILVER

Entrepreneur Press

Publisher: Entrepreneur Press
Cover Design: Andrew Welyczko
Production and Composition: Eliot House Productions

This publication is designed to provide accurate and authoritative information
in regard to the subject matter covered. It is sold with the understanding that the
publisher is not engaged in rendering legal, accounting or other professional services. If legal advice or other expert assistance is required, the services of a compe-
tent professional person should be sought.

Library of Congress Cataloging-in-Publication Data
Silver, Yanik.
   Maverick startup: 11 X-factors to bootstrap from zero to six figures (and
   beyond)/by Yanik Silver.
      p.   cm.
   ISBN-10: 1-59918-435-4 (alk. paper)
   ISBN-13: 978-1-59918-435-7 (alk. paper)
      1. New business enterprises. 2. Success in business. I. Title.
   HD62.5.S5584 2012
   658.1'1—dc23   2011048751

Printed in the United States of America

16 15 14 13 12   10 9 8 7 6 5 4 3 2 1

CONTENTS

ACKNOWLEDGMENTS

To my mom, Aleksandra, you're missed more than you realize. I've learned that one common thread among successful people has been someone who unconditionally supported them. That was my mom. And she wasn't afraid to kick back a few vodka shots either to give me a run for my money.

To my dad, Joe, you showed me what it's like to be a maverick entrepreneur before I knew I wanted to be one. To my brother, Adam, I love seeing you take the plunge into entrepreneurship with your own startup. Go ParkingPanda.com!

A big thank you goes to my wife, Missy, who has been there before I made the leap to being out on my own. You were there with the "loaned" computer from your office to help get my first idea off the ground and even a spare spot in your living room. No doubt, I was not loved by the roommates in the townhouse! And another thank you for helping create my two favorite startups, Zack and Zoe.

Countless mentors, prodders, instigators, and rabble rousers have helped in many big and small ways they might not even realize: Frank McKinney; Tony Hsieh; Joe Polish; Ryan Deiss; Dan Sullivan; Jeff Mulligan, Jeff Johnson, and Jeff Walker (or just the Jeffs); Eben Pagan; Ed Dale; Dean Jackson; Andy Jenkins; Frank Kern; Trey Smith; Perry Belcher; Tim Ferriss; Ryan Lee; Bill Harrison; Rob Olic; Chris Zavadowski; Cameron Herold; Ari Weinzweig; Dan Kennedy;

Ted Nicholas; Bill Glazer; Jim Edwards; Michael Holland; Brendon Burchard; Foster Hibbard; Earl Nightingale; Chip Conley; Sir Richard Branson; and the members of the Maverick1000 network.

Certainly my editor, Jere Calmes from Entrepreneur Press, deserves to be singled out for keeping me up late writing and making me get this book out. Thank you (I think). And to the members of our Maverick team—Andrew Way, Kim Jacobson, Aydika James, and Sophia Umanski—thanks for coming along for the ride!

And certainly I'd be remiss if I left out the individuals who actually make all of this worthwhile. My heart sings for the maverick entrepreneur who flips the bird to the status quo and decides to make an impact in a big way on their own. I owe you a drink for buying this book.

PREFACE

WHAT MAKES A MAVERICK STARTUP?

Quite simply, I believe the biggest reason we are, or want to become, entrepreneurs is the pursuit of one single ideal: FREEDOM!

I remember the only so-called real job I ever had was working at TCBY (The Country's Best Yogurt). I was 16 at the time, and working after school until close. Basically, it sucked! After a few days, free yogurt wasn't that exciting. I absolutely hated breaking down the machines at the end of the night, scrubbing the stupid tanks, and cleaning out the yogurt dispensers. Agh!!

Plus, I had to show up at the right time and leave when someone else told me to. That was the only wake-up call I needed to tell me I never wanted to be an employee again. It totally sucked and I quit.

I guess I had to get that lesson firsthand and I'm glad it didn't take me years to get it. You see, my family is one of those semi-typical immigrant success stories you hear about.

My parents arrived in the United States from Russia in 1976 with $256 in their pockets for them, my grandmother, and little Yanik. They both didn't speak much English, but they were willing to work. That "immigrant mentality" of starting from nothing and building was a driving force. My father went to work in a local hospital in their cardiology department to repair and maintain their equipment.

Very quickly, my dad started moonlighting and repairing medical equipment for some of the doctors' private practices. It wasn't too long before the hospital administrators found out about this and offered him an ultimatum: Either he stops or he gets fired.

He chose to quit and started his own business from the kitchen table of our little apartment, and grew the company to a multiple seven-figure enterprise.

It's that same spirit that pushed me to create something out of nothing (like all entrepreneurs do). But that's not all there is to the story. When I started my online businesses I decided I'd set my own criteria and make my business revolve around my lifestyle and not the other way around, not try to fit in what I enjoyed whenever I could, but actually create a business that was fun (or adding more fun to it), schedule and create time to do things on my own "Ultimate Big Life List," and make sure I was creating a massive impact through the causes I support.

You might boil down the *Maverick Startup* philosophy to this:

▶ Set your own rules
▶ Make more money
▶ Have more fun
▶ Experience a rich life
▶ And give more to make a difference

If that sounds like something you can roll with, then you're in the right place. For me, it's about the intersection of three areas of my entrepreneurial life (see Figure P.1).

And the X-Factors we'll cover inside the pages of this book are not your typical B-school advice. I graduated from a top-25 business school but I'd be hard-pressed to say I really applied my degree in any way to being an entrepreneur. Or if you came looking for some thoughts on why you should be a S Corp vs. an LLC or where to incorporate—you're barking up the wrong tree here! (There are a ton of other people that can help you there.) What you've got in front of you are some of the

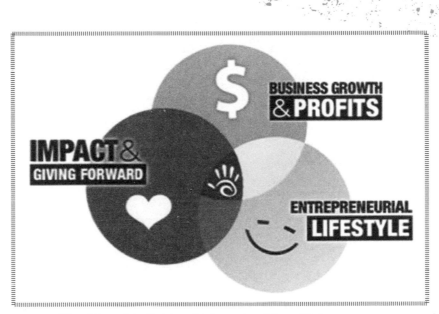

FIGURE P.1 The Maverick Startup Philosophy, Venn Style

"intangibles" that will take your budding business from a little concept on a napkin to throwing off serious revenue in a way that supports and builds up whatever else is important to you.

So turn the page, and let's get this show on the road!

X-FACTOR 1

THE BIG IDEA

IT'S GOT TO BE A BIG IDEA OR "HOOK"

I have a list of "Maverick Rules" for entrepreneurs, and this is Rule #1 in my book. I think it's got to be a BIG idea that you, your team, and your customers can "get" in seconds.

Before we get started with the how, let's talk about the why.

Why?

Easy answer is: because there is so much frickin' competition! There's just so much noise in the marketplace (in just about every marketplace) that you need some way of sticking out.

If you don't have a big idea, you simply fade into the background like every other "me-too" product or service. Actually it's not always even about having a proprietary product or service. This is really more about positioning and the immediate reaction a prospect has to your deal the moment they hear it.

That's one of the key elements of the BIG idea—gut reaction. If you want really interesting insight into this, get the book *Blink: The Power of Thinking without Thinking* by Malcolm Gladwell. You'll see exactly how much our attitudes and perceptions are based on what he calls "thin slicing." With our world being busier than ever, people usually don't have all the time in the world to explore absolutely everything about a product or service. We've got to use shortcuts for our decision making. And the clearer and more poignant you can make a distinction for your product or service, the better you'll do in the crowded marketplace.

Let me cover some real-world examples and then you'll have a little better notion of how to create the same kind of hooks and angles for yourself. I'll start with a couple of products from the consumer world and see if you can pick up on it:

▶ Uncrustables
▶ 100-Calorie Packs
▶ *8-Minute Abs*
▶ Time shares
▶ *101 Nights of Grrreat Sex*
▶ *The Real World*
▶ Club Med
▶ *24*

All of these consumer products broke out and created serious financial windfalls for the companies involved.

Uncrustables is a pretty silly idea, but it works. Create a pre-made PB&J sandwich, remove the crust, and seal it together so the bread is a little pouch. Then put in your freezer and stick in your kid's lunch bag to thaw for lunch. (Side note: We buy these a lot! My wife, Missy absolutely loves Uncrustables herself. I'm the one who loves five-star meals at fancy restaurants with great wine, while she could go for a grilled cheese sandwich any day of the week.)

100-Calorie Packs are from Nabisco and now have grown to a bunch of different varieties—anything from Ritz crackers to Oreo cookies—but they only have exactly 100 calories per pouch. That's the big idea: You don't have to count calories because we've done it for you. You know that with each snack pack you can't eat 18 portions because we've put less than 100 calories in there for you.

8-Minute Abs. The name says it all. That's all you need to hear to know exactly what you get and how long it'll take. It's specific and very powerful, enough that on the strength of this concept hundreds of thousands of copies were sold.

Time shares. It'd be almost impossible for someone today not to know what a time share is, but in the late 1960s and early '70s this was a breakthrough concept. You could simply purchase a week of a hotel/condo instead of buying the whole thing. The concept first debuted in Europe and quickly spread to the United States in Florida and Hawaii.

101 Nights of Grrreat Sex. I absolutely loved this concept when I first saw it in bookstores. It was so different. This is a paperback (mass market, bookstore) book by Laura Corn that has 50 sealed activities for men and 50 for women. You just rip out a perforated page and away you go. You don't have to think too much because it's all there for you. The other point that I absolutely love about this book is the curiosity factor. You simply cannot "browse" the book like you typically would in a bookstore. All the pages are sealed and you only get little tantalizing hints from the title of the activity like "Sucking the Mango." Laura is a fabulous marketer and constant promoter. In fact, she has also smartly charged a premium price on her book, which rings up at $29.95 (way more than most paperbacks and something we'll cover in another X-factor).

The Real World is probably the first reality TV show and was a major breakthrough because there were no actors and no script. MTV concocted a recipe to whip up mega drama from a bunch of strangers all living together. Hey, I watched it. This probably dates me a little, but I still remember season number one in New York. This concept is so strong that they are still going years and years and years later. Of course, reality TV has gone haywire in the past few years and really exploded. TV viewers will watch just about any kind of reality today.

Club Med started the all-inclusive concept for vacations in the 1950s. This was a BIG idea since previously you had to pay separately for meals, drinks, activities, etc.

24 is a TV show concept that I haven't seen copied yet. It had such a unique format with every episode occurring in an hour of real time. And the entire season occurs over exactly 24 hours. So clever. Missy and I were totally hooked on it until about the fifth or sixth season. If you watch this show, you know what I mean when I say we can't believe some of the twists and ridiculous turns the writers put in there, but we are willing go along for the ride.

FIVE WAYS TO WORK ON YOUR BIG IDEA

I want to make sure nothing is glossed over because this is critical and means the difference between a "base-hit" or a "home-run" product. What follows are five major things I think about and keep in mind when coming up with a BIG idea or hook for something I'm doing.

1. Give Them the FISH!

I can't overemphasize this idea, and I can't remember how long I've been telling this to students. People are downright lazy— cater to it! Everyone knows the saying: If you give a man a fish, you feed him for a day, but if you teach him to fish, you feed him for life. Let me give it to you straight here: That's complete and total B.S.!

People want the fish handed to them on their plate, grilled perfectly, and with some seasonal vegetables on the side. Look at Home Depot, the world's largest "do it yourself" company in the world. Why did they start buying up companies left and right and provide the service for consumers? And why does their CEO think the "done for you" services will eclipse their current sales? Hmmmm . . .

I've had big success with "giving people the fish," including the first online product I created, www.InstantSalesLetters.com. The whole hook behind Instant Sales Letters® is right in the headline on the site: "In only 2-½ Minutes You Can Quickly and Easily Create a

Sales Letter Guaranteed to Sell Your Product or Service . . . Without Writing! Looking to Increase Your Business? Just Fill in a Few Blanks and PRESTO . . . You've Just Created a Powerful, Money-Making Sales Letter!"

That hook has been responsible for my first million-dollar idea with a little $40 to $50 product.

Another big success story using the fish concept comes from our Public Domain Goldmine package created with my partner, Michael Holland. After the success of my Public Domain Riches product wherein I covered how to find and profit from public domain works, I realized many people didn't want to go through the trouble of finding the public domain works and analyzing markets themselves. Here's the big idea:

> *I'm going to hand you 35 different public domain works on a silver platter with nearly EVERYTHING done for you and ready to start making you money. We're talking all the market research, competitive analysis, keyword analysis, locating back-end affiliate revenue sources, finding potential joint venture partners, clearing the copyrights, etc. – All for a TINY fraction of the time and money you would have to spend if you did it all yourself.*

That hook was enough to make sure all the volumes released so far have instantly sold out. Giving people exactly what they want handed to them in a done-for-them concept is so powerful.

As I look back, I've been doing this since I started selling information in 1998. In fact, one of the very first successful products was a pre-done newsletter for cosmetic surgeons to send to their patients already written for them. Check out the sidebar on page 6 to see how very simple and straightforward the letter selling this product started.

One of my former students, Lisa Preston, had been struggling with the information marketing business online until she took the fish concept to heart. She ended up launching "Instant Niche Emails," which provided an easy way to get 52 weeks of follow-up autoresponders for

How to Write a Patient Newsletter. . . Without Writing

Dear Doctor,

Are you too busy to write your own patient newsletter?

You know you need a newsletter, but if you're like most doctors, you just can't find the time to ever get one out. Coming up with interesting articles and compelling stories is hard, hard work, and unless you have lots of extra time on your hands, it's easy to keep putting off publishing a newsletter until "someday."

But of course, we all know "someday" usually never comes . . .

Oh sure, there are a couple of companies that will do it all for you, but they'll charge you an arm and a leg. And since they don't really know the first thing about compelling offers and killer copy, it probably won't get too many patients to actually call you (which is the whole point of putting out a newsletter).

Well, all that can change starting now . . .

Announcing the Pre-Done, Ready-to-Go, Camera-Ready,

Just Plug in Your Name and Phone Number, Patient Newsletters!

just about any niche. It's a great concept and she quickly saw her sales explode because of the big idea.

And this isn't just for information products. If you look back over the examples I originally gave you, I would put Club Med into the fish category because they provide you everything you need to have a wonderful vacation for one price. I'd also put "Uncrustables" in the fish category since moms and dads just need to chuck one of those sandwiches into the little tyke's lunch bag and they're all set. I'd possibly even put *101 Nights of Grrreat Sex* in this since each torn-out page gives you exact specific instructions (but they don't give you all the props).

OK, on to the second way to develop BIG ideas and hooks . . .

2. Make Your Promise Specific

Specifics are so important but usually completely overlooked because it's much easier to make a generic promise. However, a specific promise or a specific target market makes your marketing that much more powerful.

One of my winners has been an e-book called *33 Days to Online Profits*, which I co-wrote with Jim Edwards. I firmly believe that "brand" has been kept alive because of the very specific claim or hook in the title. Originally when Jim and I first began discussing the idea behind this ebook it was going to be *30 Days to Online Profits*, but we decided on "33" because it was specific (and credible). The other unique aspect of this product is that each day you are given a homework assignment, so it's a step-by-step, day-by-day course for 33 days.

I have no doubt in my mind if the title was "30 Days to Online Profits" it wouldn't be as successful since 30 is a "normal" number.

Here's another example from an actual critique I gave to a student when they submitted an idea that they wanted to create as a product for stay-at-home moms. "Stay-at-home moms are a great category. You need to get specific on it, the moneymaking info. How about something like '233 Ways Stay-at-Home Moms Can Make an Extra $200 Every Month.' Now that's different, specific, and has a nice hook to it."

You can see from my comments how much more powerful this would make the concept. Specifics also apply to things like "1,001" compiled resources. However, I don't like "typical" numbers, so I'd use very specific and somewhat unusual numbers like "233" or "33" as I mentioned.

Looking back again at the first group of examples, I'd obviously put *8-Minute Abs*, "100-Calorie Packs" and probably *101 Nights of Grrreat Sex* into the specifics category. Notice how *101 Nights* is in both categories? I firmly believe you can create bigger and better hooks by having not just one of these factors in your BIG idea: Stack them on top of one another!

Another good example of specifics selling the big idea is the success of the 5-hour ENERGY® products. I first found this a few years back when I needed an energy boost before a hockey game. I went to 7-Eleven and was sitting there trying to decide which energy supplement/drink/powder/doohickey I should buy. I saw this little bottle called "5-hour ENERGY." I read a tiny bit on the back of the bottle and grabbed it. Yeah, it tasted sorta crappy, but it worked. Not only did it give me more energy (we won the championship) but it worked from their marketing standpoint.

A point-of-purchase product like that really depends on you being able to make a split-second decision whether or not you'll get it. (Fact is, many decisions are made like this from a quick, emotional, gut level, but we don't want to admit it to ourselves.) So by using a specific promise of "5 hours of energy," they were able to get my business. Now I've been seeing more and more TV commercials from them, which to me means the product has become pretty successful in a marketplace filled with competitors like Red Bull.

3. Go the Opposite Direction

I love this. However, I don't suggest being different just for the sake of being different, but there is a lot to be said for zigging when others zag.

My biggest example of this is the Underground® online seminar concept I developed.

Don't you think there are more than enough internet seminars going on all over the place? Some good. Some not so good. It's really tough to create a stir in the internet space unless you have something different. Which is exactly why I didn't want to do another same-ol' internet seminar. Of course, the easy way (and trust me, there is nothing easy about putting on seminars) would have been to just gather up all my buddies and have a seminar, but that would be too similar to other established events.

My big hook (which was true) is every year I bring in a lot of unknown speakers who were really succeeding online. It wasn't the

Join the Underground Online!

Since 2003, the Underground® Online Seminar has provided high-level internet marketing information from real-world, in-the-trenches presenters quietly making their fortunes online. It's become the top networking and learning event for internet marketers with presenting attendees such as Tony Hsieh, CEO of Zappos.com; Darren Rowse, ProBlogger.com; Bob Parsons, CEO of GoDaddy.com; Gary Vaynerchuk, author of *Crush It*; Jessica Jackley, co-founder of Kiva.org; Ted Leonsis, internet pioneer, AOL executive, and owner of the Washington Capitals and Wizards. Check out www.UndergroundOnlineSeminar.com for details on the next LIVE event.

same usual suspects you'd see at other events. I took it all the way with making the promotions "spy-themed" to stand out. Sure, some people emailed us and said it was silly. But a lot more people got into it because it was different. It really worked! Each year the event has SOLD OUT weeks before the event took place (by comparison, most other events will get the bulk of their registrants two to three weeks before the seminar and most will take registrants up until the event).

For a broader example of going the opposite direction, think about when Volkswagen Beetle first came to the U.S. with their "Think Small" campaign in 1960. It was the era of big cars and auto makers were trying to outdo themselves by building bigger and bigger cars for the American public. But the VW Beetle quickly became a blockbuster because it went in the opposite direction and even highlighted the fact it was small. This campaign was so powerful that *AdAge* magazine named it #1 in its "Top 100 Advertising Campaigns" list.

4. Move to a New Application

Many times you can create a great hook by simply taking one successful hook from one industry or place and moving it somewhere else.

A great example of this is applying the successful time shares concept I already mentioned to you to other industries. The time shares concept has been successfully applied to private jets (think NetJets), exotic cars, luxury second homes, yachts, and even vineyards.

Or, on a smaller level, one of my friends and former Underground® II speaker is a great example of this. John Alanis's site product is "Women Approach You," and the whole hook behind his info products is to get women to approach you instead of you having to chase them.

Great concept! However, it's not even close to original!

Both John and I would credit Dan Kennedy with being a tremendous influence in our business. And one of Dan's most successful products is "Magnetic Marketing," with the big idea of not chasing business but having it come to you.

See any similarities?

5. Be First

Sometimes the most important thing you can do is simply be the first. From our example list, time shares, Club Med, and MTV's *The Real World* qualify, since they were the very first in their category.

If you are moving into a crowded marketplace, you can actually "slice" off a piece of that market to be first. For instance, Dan Kennedy talks about his foray into helping dentists and chiropractors with their practice marketing. He would say his company was the single biggest provider of practice-building information for the dental and chiropractic profession. And that's because nobody else was serving both.

Or how about this one?

Hedonism (owned by SuperClubs) took the concept behind all-inclusive resorts from Club Med and geared it only toward singles or adventurous singles. But that wasn't the end, because another smart company niched the all-inclusive concept again, but only for romantic couples with their Sandals resorts.

If you start thinking about these points for creating the BIG idea or a hook, you'll begin to notice ideas everywhere. Plus, you'll also see how successful products and services are, in many ways, take-offs on other successful concepts that came before them.

How about this mega money-making example: If you have kids, you surely have heard of the Wiggles, right?

Zack likes their songs, and surprisingly (or maybe not) I now know all the words to the songs on his Wiggles CD. The Wiggles have become a huge hit by following BIG idea methods 4 and 5. So huge that according to *Business Review Weekly* magazine, the Wiggles were Australia's highest grossing entertainers for the year 2005, earning more than AC/DC and Nicole Kidman combined.

Two of the Wiggles started off in a regular rock band called the Cockroaches and had some modest success. It was only after deciding to move to a new application (Big Idea #4) and being first (Big Idea #5) did they have their massive success.

For moving to a new application, they took their same popular rock sound and moved to kids' music. Most kids' music pretty much stunk, but the Wiggles aren't bad. Now, moving to a new application they didn't need to compete against tens of thousands of other hopeful musical acts trying to go big and mainstream. They went for kids and cornered the market. According to Wikipedia, one of their hit songs came from reworking a few of the old Cockroaches tunes into children's songs. For example, "Do the Monkey" was originally a Cockroaches song with different lyrics. Another Cockroaches song, "Get Ready to Wiggle," inspired the new band's name.

Then the other portion of the BIG idea used here was #5, being first. Now, they were not literally the first children's entertainers, but they took this combination of CDs, live performance, videos, and characters to develop a sticking point in the heads of little rug rats everywhere.

"BORROWING" THE BIG HOOK OR BIG IDEA

When you see a big idea, try applying some of the following insights into borrowing it. Now notice, I didn't say "knock it off." That is the reason so many "me-too" competitors drop the ball. They don't do anything unique.

A site that's been a winner since 2004 took the complete "anti-Amazon" approach. They're called Woot.com, and they only sell one product per day until it's sold out or until midnight, when it's replaced by another item. (Funny side note: I say they took the anti-Amazon approach but were actually purchased by Amazon just recently.)

I mean, is that crazy, or what?

Not really. It's a great hook because people get it right away. In fact, there have been a whole lot of sites trying to knock off this idea. Most aren't able to make theirs work because they are competing in the same space. Big mistake.

You can easily transport one big idea to another industry or niche, but trying to compete in the same space is usually disaster because the first person in gets the recognition. One of my previous Millionaire MasterMind members has a site just for software for Macs. Now that's smart, because it's this proven concept, but niched out.

Woot.com themselves just branched out to the niche of wine and opened wine.woot.com. I'm not sure if this will be as profitable as the electronics and gizmos side of their site because of the inherent problems wine has (high shipping cost, cannot ship to all states, fragile shipment, etc.), but it shows good creativity. They are taking their own successful concept and leveraging that success.

As you were reading this, maybe you thought about Groupon.com, the fastest company to reach a billion-dollar valuation. They certainly took the concept of the deal-a-day similar to Woot.com and really leveraged it. More about Groupon later on too.

A brand-new site that's just launched, which seems partially based on the Woot.com concept but still has its unique spin, is 20ltd.com.

This site sells items that are unique to 20ltd.com and only 20 items at a time and in limited editions. They are appealing to an ultra-luxury, upscale marketplace.

Will this work?

Maybe, but once again at least this is not the same ol', same ol,' so it definitely has a chance of working. Plus, the rarity and scarcity of the items doesn't hurt. You never know when you might want a £9,000 cashmere and black fox fur hammock for your backyard.

The more you can incorporate a BIG idea or hook into your product, the easier it'll be to write a kick-ass sales promotion for it. It almost writes itself. The times when I've struggled writing copy is because I didn't have enough of a big idea behind it.

X-Factor 2

YOUR VISION

WHAT DO YOU REALLY, REALLY WANT?

Creating a compelling and inspiring vision is the key to making sure you get where you want to go, and your team is behind you. This is how you know what to say "Yes" to and, more importantly, what to say "No" to.

Quite frankly, when I first got started in business, I thought the ideas of "visions" and "mission statements" were pretty much bullshit. Just stuff that looked really good framed next to a bathroom.

But I've had two people greatly influence me in this regard (so much so that it's actually X-Factor 2). The first person is my friend, Cameron Herold. Cameron was the former COO of 1-800-Got-Junk and helped the company grow from $2 million to $105 million in revenue in six years with no debt or outside shareholders, an awesome achievement by any standard.

Maverick Resource

For a few more insights, read Cameron's blog and search for the "Painted Picture" category: www. backpocketcoo.com/blog.

One of the "secrets" to his success is having a "Painted Picture," a document that gives a vivid description of what your company looks and acts like at a certain time in the future. I'll show you an example of my Painted Picture at the end of this chapter.

The other mentor who has been a big influence in this area for me is Ari Weinzweig, co-founder of Zingerman's. I recently attended a conference and had the opportunity to connect with Ari. I had heard and read a bit about Zingerman's approach to business and knew it was interesting and different, but didn't realize how unusual it really was until I dug in.

I attended Ari's breakout session, had a few conversations with Ari, read his new book called *A Lapsed Anarchist's Approach to Building a Great Business* (highly recommended), started researching them, etc. And the more I saw, the more I really loved how they built their business, the philosophy, the culture, and more, so I knew I had to ask Ari for an interview.

ZINGERMAN'S BACK STORY

It all started as a simple deli in Ann Arbor, Michigan, in 1982, with a co-founder, Paul Saginaw. The notion was to give local residents real, authentic deli food and never skimp on the quality. Over the next decade, Zingerman's deli grew because their food was a hit, but they hit a plateau at about $5 million in revenue. It was at that point they came up with an ingenious plan for creating growth without sacrificing the elements of being a small business in a community they loved. In fact, Ari was adamant that he would not expand Zingerman's deli to a bunch of other cities, attempt to duplicate the ambience, and create some mediocre version of what they started.

THE POWER OF VISIONING A POSITIVE FUTURE

Instead, in 1992 Ari and Paul wrote out their vision for 2004. It was to have a group of 10 to 12 small businesses, referred to as Zingerman's Community of Businesses or ZCoB.

And that's exactly what happened. Each one would bear the Zingerman's name but have its own unique identity and specialty, including everything from a bake shop to a mail order facility to a training and seminar company teaching the "secret sauce" to their success.

Even though Ari loathes citing one secret for Zingerman's success (and truthfully, there is never just one factor), getting good at visioning is something they do everywhere in the organization, so there's got to be something to that. He says,

> One of the biggest contributors to the level of creativity in our organization is the regularity with which we teach, use, and stick to the visioning process. We start pretty much every planning effort with a draft of a positive vision of the future. And we do it at every level of the organization. Whether we're working on visions for a business five years out, a project that will be done in five months, or a dinner special that will be on the menu at 5:00 tonight, we're pretty consistently "beginning with the end in mind."

In fact, it's been proven that when people use visioning instead of simply problem solving, energy levels increased, innovative ideas flowed, and people were excited and eager about their future. What's more, visioning also gets you clear on what you do NOT want to do in your business so that you can easily turn down seemingly golden opportunities that come your way (this is the reason why Ari and Paul always said no to creating franchises or other locations outside Ann Arbor.)

I've included a bonus interview for you here.

ARI WEINZWEIG INTERVIEW:
HOW TO DEVELOP YOUR IDEAL VISION FOR
YOUR GREAT BUSINESS AND PERFECT FUTURE

YANIK: All right, well, I'm really excited. I saw your breakout session INC500, read the book. I've been raving about that, bought it for some of our key people here—*A Lapsed Anarchist's Approach to Building a Great Business*. You know, when I first met you, I told you, Ari, I read a little bit about you guys. *INC* magazine called you guys the coolest small company in America. So you guys are doing some really exciting things over there and unfortunately we only have an hour together.

I wish we had even more time because there are so many things we can cover. But I really want to zero in on the visioning part because you take a couple of chapters in your book to cover it. I know you always talk about people asking you, "OK, what's the secret to Zingerman's success," and it's not just one thing, it's so many different things you guys do. But you guys talk about how this is a part of everything that goes on. So what's your introduction to visioning, or maybe, give us a snapshot of 1982 to where you guys are today and then we'll touch on visioning for a second afterwards.

ARI: OK, sounds great. So, yeah, 1982, let's see. I grew up in Chicago; I came up to Ann Arbor to go to school like lots of people. I studied Russian history with particular interest in anarchists, which has now come back in the form of the book. And after I graduated I pretty much knew I didn't want to go home but I didn't really know what else I was going to do and I knew I needed a job in order to make that financially viable. I did not grow up in any kind of family business setting. Everybody in my family were all lawyers, doctors, academics, and I didn't grow up with any passion for food or anything, either.

But one of my roommates was waiting tables at a restaurant here in town and it sounded like a good place to work. So I went in there looking for a job and I waited two, three weeks till they had something open, and the only thing they had open was washing dishes. But I needed the money, so I took the job. And I feel incredibly fortunate, because I stumbled into this line of work that I really love. I mean, I really had no intention of getting into food or into business at all. But one of the essays in the book is "Twelve Natural Laws of Business," and one of the natural laws is that success means you get better problems, and a good problem I have is there's nowhere near enough years left to do all the things that I want to do, but I also stumbled into great people.

So Paul Saginaw, who you mentioned, is my partner, but he was the general manager of the restaurant. And I stayed and worked with that company for about four years. I started prepping, line cooking, managing kitchens, and gave a couple of months' notice—and actually it would be 29 years ago this week as a matter of fact. And Paul happened to call me like two days later, and we talked off and on about doing a deli together. And the building where the deli is now was coming open, and he said we should go down and check it out, so we did, and we opened up four and a half months later.

YANIK: And it's one of those kind of—people look at it as an overnight success story but took years in the making to become that.

ARI: Overnight, over 29 years of overnight. We're still working at It, never done. But trying to get better and keep learning and have fun.

YANIK: And there's a point when, you discuss this in the book, and the story goes you guys were kind of up to your elbows with all sorts of stuff going on in the deli, and Paul called you out and he said, "Hey Ari, where do you want to be?" and I think you said ten years from now, right?

ARI: Yeah. When we opened, I mean we didn't actually call it a vision then. We didn't have that terminology, but in essence we had a pretty clear vision. We knew from the beginning that we only wanted one deli and that we weren't going to try to open a chain of them. We didn't want to replicate it, we really like unique things. We knew we wanted someplace that was in that context unique to Ann Arbor that wasn't a copy of something from New York or Chicago or Los Angeles or Detroit.

We knew that we wanted a great place for people to work and a place that customers can come in and get amazing food and service but in a really accessible setting and have something that really provides a great work opportunity and really be grounded in the community. And for context, I mean when we opened, and I'm sure most of the people who are followers of yours would've had similar stories, but of course everybody told us it would never work. Ann Arbor had a dozen delis fail in the previous decade.

The spot where the deli is is very hard to find. I mean today it's not hard with cell phones and GPS. But up until five, six years ago, it was a pretty fairly convoluted series of one-way streets you got to go down to get there. There's no parking, and the neighborhood was considered a bad neighborhood. So of course we went ahead and opened, and six, seven years later, everybody told us we were brilliant, it's a great location. So anyway, by probably early '90s, you know, we "were successful" by traditional terms.

We expanded twice on that site. We've been written up in *The New York Times*. We've been in *Bon Appetit, Gourmet*, and all that stuff. But again, I'm sure many of your listeners can relate. We weren't rich. We weren't retiring. We were doing well, but it's sort of like, what do we do now? And our original vision had been just of the one place and we couldn't really expand anymore on that site; we're in a historic district. And like you said, Paul sort of grabbed me one morning and set me down out in front of the deli and he said, "So OK, in ten years, what are we doing?" and I really had no interest in having that conversation.

I just wanted to go in and get set up for lunch, but he kept pushing on me. He said, "Come on, I mean, we have this commitment to only have one, but we're turning down offers from other cities to open there. You know people are opening on campus now and they're starting to eat into our market. Are we really owning it, what are we doing?" And I'm like, "Paul, man, I just want to get ready for lunch; we're going to get busy here," and to his credit he kept pushing on me and we ended up staying. It really was like a yearlong dialogue because it's really not that easy, your question, to answer.

When you say what you don't want and it's easy to say what you might change tomorrow, but if somebody actually says, "Well, go ahead, paint a picture, what are you doing in ten years? How much money do you make? How big is the company? What do you do when you go to work? How do people feel about the workplace?" I mean it's the theory of it in that art, but when somebody sort of challenges you to actually write it down, it's a little scary for somebody like me. For Paul, I think it's more intuitive. I'm more of the type that I don't want to tell you what I want to do till I know I can do it well.

But anyway, he kept pushing on me, and like I said, we stayed in that conversation for a solid year, which included lots of agreement, lots of disagreement, lots of eye-rolling, I'm sure plenty of swear words, and some other stuff. But by the end of about a year we came out with a new vision that we called Zingerman's 2009, and so it was actually 15 years out into the future. And it outlined what you described, a community we would call Zingerman's Community of Businesses. We would grow, instead of using the traditional model of opening more delis, we would grow by opening other Zingerman's businesses here in the Ann Arbor area.

We only would do stuff in this area because we like to be connected to the community and we like to know the people working with us, and know the customers, and that each business would have a managing partner or partners in it. And so these are people who actually put money in and really, literally own part of that business and that would be driving it for greatness every day. And we would operate as one organization with these autonomous pieces where really the organization overall would be greater than some of the individual parts. As with the original vision, really nobody liked it. The long-time deli managers, to their credit, had worked hard to really solidify things there and stabilize them, and now we were talking about sort of going back to acting like a startup again.

The business school model hates us because we're not replicating what we're good at, and you are supposed to stay in your core competency all the time. And I still haven't figured out how you are supposed to get a core competency if you only do things you're good at. You have to by definition have been bad at something to get going. And the accountants don't like it because the businesses sell back and forth to each other and pretty much it was not really well-received in the moment. And then you mentioned Bo Burlingham's article in *INC* and we were on the cover of *INC* and all of a sudden we were geniuses again and now it's a model all these other people want to copy and stuff.

So that was that, and then in 2006 we realized we were getting awful close to this vision, which once seemed like six lifetimes away, was now basically kind of done and we realized we better write the next one. So we spent about a year and a half this time with all the managing partners. So consensus decision making by which is how we operate at that level of all the managing partners plus 60 different people, and got input from over 250 people in the organization and finished that in 2007, and that's our 2020 vision, which is in the book, as is the other one.

YANIK: Yeah, right, and well, people should definitely check that out inside the book because it's a great example of the big, overarching vision. And one of the things you talked about was how the other visions in the business would kind of cascade down from that overarching one. But what I want to bring you back to and something that I don't know if it's in the book or I saw it in an article on you guys was I think it mentioned that 85 percent of your managers or people left, or 75 percent left after, at that . . .

ARI: Yeah, I mean, it wasn't that. We probably had the eight or nine managers, and most of them over the two years that followed the introduction of the vision left. You know, having read about it from other people, it's not an uncommon thing. It's not anything bad.

You got people who we had brought in, in the interest of sort of making things run smoothly, and they had worked hard to make that happen and it had gotten to where they didn't have to work every weekend and all the stuff that you got to do in the startup. And then all of a sudden here we were changing the model on them. It was a slow process, and they all left on good terms and some of them we buy from now, or they're all regular customers or whatever, but yeah, it wasn't the most fun part of it.

YANIK: Yeah, I know. I just point that out as something you guys stuck to, to that vision, and that was even when you're seeing what other people might consider adverse effects of the management leaving and so forth. But let's talk about maybe a little bit why do you think—let's define that vision. So you mentioned a little bit what it is. It's literally sitting down and us figuring out what is our ideal or whatever the end goal looks like, and why do you think it works?

ARI: Well, the basic idea of visioning is as you just said. It's very clear to the point of actually writing down what your future success looks like. A couple of things that it isn't, I guess, just to give context, is, it's not a mission statement. We have a mission statement and I wrote about that in the book, also, and we're big believers in that. But the mission statement for us, it's sort of like the North Star.

I always talk about delivering a great Zingerman experience to people, and we take that very seriously, but it doesn't really define, you know, it's sort of a broad stroke, like the North Star; you can find it every day but it doesn't actually say what you're going to do. Our vision also is not a strategic plan. We also do strategic planning. But strategic planning as we view it is how you get from the present-day reality to the vision. And I still can't quite figure out how everybody does strategic plans, but they don't agree on a vision, because the vision is where you're ultimately going.

So the vision—that's really what it is—I mean, it just describes success and it needs to be written down so that other people can understand it. And it starts to get into a lot more detail that is not stuff that's typically included in people's plans. It could include how the employees feel about working there. It could include how the community feels about the business being in it. It would certainly include in some ways what you and I as the owner would be doing or how much we're making.

And it doesn't need to be like to the nth degree of detail, but just a sense of scale and scope that really start to give clarity around where you're headed. So our 2020 vision says that by 2020 we will have 12 to 18 Zingerman businesses all in the Ann Arbor area here. That's not 120 and it's not 10. So we're not trying to narrow it down so much that we can't move, but an organization with 100 businesses is radically different than one with 15, and it allows us to be clear about what we're doing.

When we get calls—which we do all the time—of people, you know, "Come open in Washington, DC," "Come open in Las Vegas," come open here or there. It's a very simple answer because we already know we're not doing it. Our vision's written out and this is what we're going to do and that means everybody in the organization knows that, when they come on board, that's what they're getting into and it gives them a sense of where they're going.

YANIK: There's a couple of really big things in there that you mentioned. One was that the vision gives you an opportunity to say no to things because as entrepreneurs we always seem like there's so many opportunities going on and that if we don't say yes to it that we're missing out on something.

ARI: Absolutely, and that's huge. I mean, most of the world—and this is how I was raised too; it's nothing bad about it. But most of the world is trained to respond to opportunities and problems when they arise, and this is actually the opposite. This is where you're—and I'm not ignoring completely, but you're basically tuning out the momentary situation and you're going after a positive future.

YANIK: Yeah, and you were talking about when you bring in people, they know where you guys are going. And I think this also helps you bring in great people who are inspired by the vision and who want to be a part of where you're going.

ARI: Yeah, there's no question. This comes up in the book over and over again, and it's a huge piece of what we do, but we're certainly not the only ones who realize this. But I think everybody really wants to be a part of something that's greater than them; it's just human nature. The vision really is the cathedral that we're building as an organization, and I share this story in the book, which I didn't make up, and I honestly can't remember where I heard it, but others would have heard it somewhere else.

But it's a story of a guy walking through the construction site of the cathedral in Milan in Italy, and he comes up to one guy and he says, "What are you doing?" and the guy says, "I'm laying stone." And he walks further along and he comes to the second guy and he says, "Well, what are you doing?" and he says, "I'm building a cathedral." And obviously the hands-on work is the same. Obviously the emotional context is radically different, and I think that people want to contribute to something great.

The reality is your job, my job, and most people's jobs, day to day, hour to hour, is fairly repetitive. But what makes the difference is that we understand that we're actually constructing something special. And I think that most entrepreneurs have that in their mind; it's just as you hire other people, they don't know what that cathedral is, and pretty soon it just becomes sort of the day-to-day drudgery in working for a check instead of it creating something amazing.

YANIK: Yeah, let's dig into it a little bit and then talk about you having an eight-step formula that's certainly outlined in the book. I think it gives people some nuts and bolts to get going on it. The first one is just the belief in the process.

ARI: Yeah, that's the thing of having done this now for many years, there's no question. I've realized that this is actually the ingredients for doing it. If you don't believe in it, it's not going to work. And I'm not trying to be all mystical and magical about it, but it's really true of anything. If you put any change in place and you don't believe in it, you can get it moving but the reality is not a lot of good stuff is going to come out of it.

YANIK: And then, I guess, part of that also is you talked about it took a year back and forth to come up with a 2009 vision and a while to come up with a

2020 one. Now you might be thinking, "My God, I don't have a year to come up with what my vision is!" In this eight-step formula you don't need a year.

ARI: You can do it in 20 minutes. It's just like, in this case, you have two partners—me and Paul—and we didn't, when we started. Sort of like you live with somebody in a house for ten years, right, then all of a sudden, you move to a new house and you find yourself having arguments over where the couch goes, or I can't believe you want to put the stove there. It's stuff that for years you never even questioned it, and we had gone along with this one basic vision that we had started with, and then all of sudden it's like you got this completely blank slate.

You got two different humans, and the key was to keep coming back to the table until we came to an agreement. When we wrote the most recent one, that's 16 partners, all of whom have their own opinions, and lives, and passions, and whatever. And trying to get the work to get them all together is not an overnight thing while you're running a business and doing everything else. But absolutely, you can sit down and draft a vision, I think, in half an hour.

YANIK: These eight steps will get you there or at least a good way there. Number two, you said, is your gut, and I think that's really true.

ARI: Yeah, these are the ingredients. We'll get to the actual recipe in a minute, but the whole thing of visioning and the way this works is I believe actually the opposite of the way most of the world works. So the sort of—I'm stereotyping—but the standards of the business school model is, you're supposed to figure out what the public wants and how you are going to make a lot of money. And there's nothing wrong with that, but this is completely the opposite.

This is going with your gut, what's your passions, what do you want to do, what gets you excited, and the whole thing of the vision is there's no right answer. It's really what you want to do. You want to bring your dog to work? Then start a business where your dog can come to work. If you want to have your kids at work, do that. If you want to travel, write a vision for a business where you're traveling all the time, and really, the whole thing is about really a sustainable life and a sustainable business.

I mean, there's no right answer for how much money is the right amount of money. Some people are happy with 5,000, some want 50,000, and some want 500,000. They're all okay, but you need different businesses to get to the higher levels than you do at the lower level. So it's all really about getting in touch with where you're at as a starting point, and work from the inside out, as opposed to working from the outside in and trying to do what other people tell you how to do.

YANIK: Yeah, and then just a couple of other ingredients and then we'll move into the steps.

ARI: Yeah, sure. The time thing you mentioned, you know, like I said, it can be done, I'm really not joking; in a half hour you can draft an amazing vision, it just depends on how many people. You got to get involved, and when you got, like we did, more than one equity owner, it's not just one person sitting down on their own and doing it. The fourth ingredient is just the willingness to kind of make yourself vulnerable.

I think instinctively for me it's awkward just because my nature is like, "Well, damn, I don't know if I want to tell everybody that this is really what I'm dreaming." We might fail, it might not work, and so you really kind of have to put yourself out there. And when one is following along with what the marketplace is telling you or whatever, you can always blame the marketplace or the consultant. In this case, it's really coming from inside your own spirit and your own soul or your own brain or whatever word you want to use, so we're sort of out there.

The good thing is I think it's a willingness or readiness to do something great. This isn't about playing it safe, and I don't mean safe gamble on a lot of money. It's just if you want to work six months a year in Hawaii, then write a vision that says you're operating from Hawaii six months a year. It's really just going after something special and meaningful; again, the idea that it's about building an amazing cathedral.

YANIK: And then, obviously, the getting it to completion, of getting it on paper and getting it out there.

ARI: And then just sticking with the process. I really, I can't tell you, I love them, but I got a lot of friends who start this and they never finish it. It's just if you stick with it and you finish it and you roll it out to your organization and you get them bought in it would happen. And honestly, we do visions for each of our businesses.

We do visions for every project, and I'm sure I'm forgetting some. But for the most part almost every single one we've ever written and actually redone, we've done it. It's not always easy getting there and there's always the challenges, and you know the economy is going to tank, or people leave, or whatever, but in the end we get there.

YANIK: So that's interesting. We'll definitely come back to that, and if we spend a little time on the reverse-engineering parts, I think that would be important. All right, so let's get with the recipe in food terms because it's great: in the ingredients, recipe—there you go.

ARI: So again, we do visioning for everything, so if we got a new product that we're working on, we do a vision. If we're starting a new whatever, a project by selling our cheese at the farmers market, we write a vision. So really, everybody in the organization is learning visioning.

This isn't just something that we're doing at the partner level. Every new whatever, 17-year-old busboy is sitting in classes where they're learning about visioning. So real simple, the first thing is pick your topic, so for many people that might mean your entire organization, but for some it could just be your personal life. It could be a project that they want to take on, it could be their summer home. And the second step is to pick your time frame.

YANIK: One thing that you mentioned, and I think people will appreciate this: Before we got started live, you said some of them were as little as one to three paragraphs.

ARI: Oh, yeah, absolutely, a vision for a small project could literally be a paragraph, and this is years of us doing it now. But it's so in our culture that literally the server would say to a managing partner, "Hey, dude, where's your vision, come on, man," which I think is great, because it means that we've institutionalized it. It's built into the culture where front line people will call out leaders because every leader knows, we screw up every day.

It's really a great service to us when we're helped by the organization to pick up the pace if we start to slack. So yeah, small project, small vision. It could be a paragraph. It could be two paragraphs, whatever, and literally when you get good at this you learn to go with your gut, which isn't easy if you got years of experience of being trained out of going with your gut. But you go with your gut and you get used to doing it; it's ten minutes, it's no big deal.

YANIK: And step two.

ARI: Step two is to pick a time frame. So for an organization overall, you know, we're just working on a new long-term vision for a mail-order business, we've been doing it since the early '90s. We've actually reached the stage there somewhat like we did at the deli in the early '90s. We kind of done what we need to do and it's time to write a new vision and in this case we got a fair amount of changes going on, and so we're doing it only three years out.

But typically we would probably do five at the least, for a business as much as ten. There's no right time frame, but the point is to get far enough out that it's not tomorrow, unless it needs to be done tomorrow, and not so far that people don't have any sense of it. But we like to go longer than shorter. For a small project, it might be a year or six months, something like that.

YANIK: Cool. Step three is put together what you call a list of "prouds."

ARI: Yeah, just the whole thing of visioning, really. I'm sure there's probably biblical origins of it, but the modern work actually coincidentally was done here at the University of Michigan by Eddie Ron Lippitt in the late '60s and '70s, and they called it Preferred Futuring. And they did a lot of work around studying group dynamics and group energy levels. And they did a study where they put some groups in to do traditional problem solving. You know, where sales are low on this and we want you guys to come up with some solutions.

What they found was, after serving a quick burst of energy with ideas, then what happened—we've all been at those meetings—pretty soon everybody says, "Well, that will never work, and that would never work, and we tried this," and pretty soon they're bogged down, and the energy just really starts to drop really low. Then they flipped it around and they took similar groups and they said, "Well, don't even worry about the way it is now. We want you to just plan yourself five years in the future, just describe what success looks like, forget the present-day problems, forget all the constraints in the moment, and just describe your success."

And then all of a sudden, they found the energy went up, creativity went up, buying went up, and the whole thing of this is to focus on the positives and what you want and what you believe in and what feels good. So, before we start the visioning process, we generally like to start by, just like you said, listing our successes, or it could be personal successes. It could be organizational successes. But it just sort of gets people thinking about, like, these are the tools that you already have in place that are working and they are all tools you can put into play in the new vision.

YANIK: Yeah, I know it helps. I've done that in my personal journal. I've done it with our company. That helps a lot with people. Instead of naturally going to what's wrong, they are forced to focus on the positive.

ARI: Yeah, you know, look, I was raised to focus on what's wrong, and it's not inherently evil, it's just not real motivating for most people.

YANIK: Yeah, exactly. All right. What's the next step then?

ARI: The fourth step would be that you actually start writing your vision. I literally would suggest timing it, and I wouldn't spend more than a half an hour on the first draft. It's really about going with your gut. The way that we do it is you sit down at the computer with a piece of paper or whatever works and just start writing. We call it hot pen, which basically means you just start writing and just keep going.

Don't edit it, don't worry about whether your mother's going to like it, your business school professor is going to like it, your accountant's going to like it, don't worry about what *The Wall Street Journal* is going to say, just go with it and really push the envelope to go for something great and write from the heart. You know there's no right ways. For me and Paul, doing something really unique is more important than making more money. So that's what's in ours, but for other people it could be more important to need more money; there's no rights or wrongs.

You write "Draft" at the top of it because it is a draft. That gives you the freedom, I think, or at least gives me the freedom, to just throw stuff down there that's completely off the wall. You can always take it out later. But I found at least for myself and most people when you start to self-edit, you start cutting out many of the things that make you excited, but you start going, "How are we going to do that? We'll never be able to do this. My partner would never go for that," and it really limits it. So it's really just sit down, start writing, and go 15 to 30 minutes.

YANIK: Yeah, and I love that technique of writing "Draft" on there. I think it's huge because that does give you permission and then it kind of turns off that internal editor we all have.

ARI: Yeah, absolutely . . . we've done this so many times, and I just guarantee if you just start writing, stuff comes out. And sometimes it's stuff that's just below the surface and you kind of knew it. And sometimes it's deeper all the time it happens. I'll write something that I'm kind of joking and then I go back and look at it and I'll go, "Well, you know, I actually want that." I just threw it down there sort of making fun of myself for whatever and then I really—nine times out of ten I'm like, "You know what? That is actually what I would like to do."

YANIK: Awesome. All right, and then what's next?

ARI: Well, the fifth step is: Just give yourself a little time and whatever, a day or two to sort of let the dust settle, pull out the draft and reread it and see how it goes. You know, there's no rights or wrongs. For me, at least at this point, I find it almost always even when I thought the draft was completely crazy, it actually turns out to be pretty right on. If you're doing this with . . . two partners, frequently what we'll do is each partner will just do this process on their own and then come together with a draft. You know, to share the draft, and then you can pull out common themes and start to carry it forward, which is what we did with the mail order one the other day and we're going to take three or four months to work on it.

YANIK: That's interesting. So would you use it that way if people are almost like 50/50 partners, or would you have let's say somebody's a majority partner?

ARI: Well, it doesn't really matter. We use consensus at the partner level regardless of who owns what. I'm not saying other people need to do that, that's just what we do. But the more people you get involved, the better the value is going to be, the longer it takes. But by the time we were done with the 2020 vision, it really belonged to everybody in the organization, and that's a pretty cool thing. And you're going to get input; it's through the owner like I am or you or whatever. You got to have your stuff in there because it's got to get you excited. But it's amazing what happens when you start to incorporate small things that other people feel strongly about and let them get a little piece of it, because it becomes their cathedral, too.

YANIK: Yeah. One of my buddies, Brendon Burchard, he has a quote he likes, it's, "People support what they create."

ARI: Yeah, that's totally true.

YANIK: And it makes a lot of sense. OK, so what happens after?

ARI: Well, the sixth step is two or three more redrafts. You can sort of keep going a little bit on your own, but my feeling is that trying to get to the first redraft on your own, it's time to start showing it to other people. Yeah, and we call those ACEs, or Advisory Content Experts. You can call them whatever you want, but the idea is to get people who kind of understand you, who think somewhat similarly. I don't mean they're not going to give you structured criticism, but I wouldn't take it to the biggest cynic or the most conservative thinker on your block right off, because hopefully you've put your heart and soul into this thing and you made yourself a little vulnerable by putting stuff down there that's a little crazy-seeming to your average human. And so I would suggest going to people who share whatever entrepreneurial passions, who are out-of–the-box thinkers or whatever, and start to get their input, and you don't have to do what they say. It's going to help you start to shape the vision and make it more robust.

YANIK: What about when some of those ACEs or somebody else from the organization starts saying, "Well, that can't happen," or that becomes more of a factor?

ARI: Well, you have to decide. I mean, this is the challenge. Paul and I sort of come to realize that usually if we're doing something great it generally means most people aren't going to like it. So we sort of have a little informal joking pact with each other, when everybody tells us it's a good idea, we start to get nervous. When they all start telling us it would never work. we go, "Great, we're on to something really good!" but that's a challenge. There's no way to know, and that's one of the risks of anything in life, really, is you don't know if it's going to work. And I think most of us are trained to play it fairly seemingly conservative. We don't think it's conservative, but it kind of is because it's just going along one day at a time. And I don't mean people aren't doing any planning, but to actually put yourself out there ten years from now and say how much money is enough money, say what kind of place you want to be at when you walk in the door, or how you want it to feel—that's a little harder.

YANIK: Yeah, all right, so let's wrap up the steps.

ARI: Yeah, the eighth one is actually to start going. At some point you actually decide this is what we're going to use. It is because it's written down, it's out there. We go over it in every new staff orientation, and everybody here has seen it, and it's out there to whatever, for people to take pot shots, or like any long-term project, there's going to be days where it feels like a failure en route.

But for us, it's like we got this diagram or architectural drawings of this cathedral that we're going to be building over a long period of years and we just keep working at it and keep it moving. And every year we do strategic planning that will take us a couple years out but we don't have the plan that goes all the way to 2020. So basically the vision is, we describe it as sort of like the "what the future looks like," and the strategic planning which we do after that is sort of the how we're going to get there. And each year we do a few years of that, but there's still a gap in between. Let's say at this point 2012 or 2013 and 2020.

YANIK: OK, so sharing it, like how widely do we distribute it? Do you get it out to your vendors? Do you get it out to your customers? Do you get it out to everyone?

ARI: Well, that's a decision you can make. We're mostly focused on sharing with people within the organization. You know, vendors certainly doesn't hurt. If you have an accountant, and a really good accountant, or a really good lawyer, they need to be more than just sort of filling in a checklist for you. In our minds, it's critical that they understand what we're doing and why we're doing what we're doing so that they can design their work in order to support it. So there's no risk. I think that truly the fact that our vision is unique and it has us staying here in the Ann Arbor area, etc., etc. You know, customers do know what it is and I think that that has increased loyalty because they know we're not going public, they know we're not franchising. They know that they are a part of something special, too, and I think that customer loyalty certainly is driven a lot by that.

YANIK: One of the things that I noticed when I read your 2020 and your 2009 vision, that it is was almost story-based.

ARI: Well, it is, because that's what it is. It's not just a bunch of bullet points. It's painting a picture that, when a new employee sits down and reads it I want him to be excited that they get to work on it. When I reread it, I want to be excited that I get to work on it because it's a lot of years of work.

YANIK: Yeah.

ARI: And I'm no different than anybody else. I mean, as motivated as everybody who's listening to this show, I'm sure, is, we all got the days where we don't want to get out of bed, or the days that we don't want to deal with one more unhappy customer, or one more employee who wants to tell you what's wrong with your organization or whatever. For me, having that vision clear up where I'm going is a huge help.

YANIK: You said you guys take that out of your strategic plan each year. Do you read that or revisit it every so often? Have you ever changed your vision that you've written?

ARI: We don't change the vision. I don't mean you can't, but if you change the vision every two years, then ten years out you're sort of defeating the purpose. So there's four characteristics that we list of an effective vision, which again are in the book. One is it needs to be inspiring, this is sort of the cathedral thing. The second is it needs to be strategically sound, and this comes back to your question when people are telling you it's crazy. A great vision is going to be some modicum of balance between: so inspiring it sounds slightly crazy, but still strategically doable.

If it's a no-brainer, it's not very inspiring even though it's shaped. If it's super inspiring but if you have no chance of getting there, we call that a fantasy, which is also nice but not the same as a vision. So it needs to be inspiring, it needs to be strategically sound. The third thing is it does need to be documented. Putting it in writing, I just tell you, it has an enormous power, and I think that most successful entrepreneurs actually have a vision, but most of us have it in their head. I would tell you it is radically different when it is written down and everybody you work with sees it, reads it, and in a good way they hold us accountable for it.

And then the fourth thing is what we were just talking about: you got to communicate it. People need to know what it is, and we go over it with everybody. Anybody that's getting interviewed or hired really is brought up to speed on that vision, because if somebody comes to work here and they're thinking ahead, and want to move up in the organization, and are thinking they're going to open a Zingerman's in Chicago when we franchise, [they're] going to be severely frustrated and disappointed when they find out. If they don't know upfront, they're going to be mad later when they find out we are not doing it.

YANIK: So does everybody in the organization see it just that one time, then, for the annual strategic planning session, or?

ARI: The vision, oh, no. It's all over. It's in the handbook. It's on the internet. And I don't know that they can recite every single part of it, but they all know what's going on because every day somebody walks up to the chief counter at the deli or they're sitting down at a table at the roadhouse, or whatever, or they're on the phone with mail order and they're going to say stuff like, "Hey, you guys got to open in like Denver," and everybody who works here can give them a constructive answer and knows what the answer is. So it's not like they have to call corporate to find out what the response is supposed to be.

YANIK: The fact that everyone in the team has been trained on visioning and you guys will do even simple things for visioning—where does that live, or where do they go so that people can keep referencing them?

ARI: They're all over the place. I'm sure in some way we should probably have some central repository, but I mean there's just thousands of them. At any given day I might get two or ten on email just from whatever, even a hot chocolate recipe.

YANIK: You said a hot chocolate recipe?

ARI: Oh, yeah, because it's the same—the customer feels about the hot chocolate, you know, is it a good margin item. These are all in there when you start to write into the vision. How do the customers react when we make the change? How do the employees feel? And then they'll just throw all of that in there.

YANIK: That's interesting. You know, one of the hot buttons I guess that you talked about was for an owner to put in how much is enough of their money and their vision. So you're totally comfortable with that? I mean I guess you guys do the open-book finance and stuff.

ARI: Well, yeah. We don't have—and they're exactly what it is. You can write parts of it that are personal and take them out of the one that you published. But at least, for yourself to know, because we made decisions that we are not going public and that we are not going to franchise and that there's trade-offs and we are good with those trade-offs. But it precludes that we're going to get this big windfall of money. It's not going to come, and we're fine with that, but somebody else might want to make $2 million a year; it's nothing wrong with that. It's just you can't do what we're doing and make $2 million a year.

YANIK: Gotcha. Well, talk about one of the things that I thought was profound that you mentioned earlier, that you guys have hit almost every single vision. That just blows me away. So what's your process for the reverse engineering aspect of it? How do we take our vision to then make it a reality among our team?

ARI: Well, actually, it would be in the next book; it's not in this book, but we have the whole process for organizational change that we teach in our vision training seminars and internal classes that's called "Bottom-Line Change," and visioning is part of that. And one of the steps is that you actually get everybody that's going to be impacted to sit together and write out the action plan, which you can call it strategic planning or whatever, and those are the action steps.

We screw all this stuff up too just like everybody else; it's not like it runs perfectly. Just today we are going to a partner meeting and they're trying to figure out how to resolve a certain issue and somebody said, "Well, where's the vision? Did they write a vision on this?" And somebody said, "Yeah, we did," and somebody else said, "Well, where is it?" and then like, "I'll send it back out again tomorrow."

YANIK: Right, so it comes back, too.

ARI: Yeah, it's not like we don't start down the same roads everybody else does. It's just that this is years of working at it, but the self-discipline sort of comes up, or somebody immediately goes, "Well, didn't we write a vision?" and somebody else would say, "Yes, I have it." OK, well, let's not waste any more time on it, then. Next time we meet we'll go over the vision.

YANIK: Right, right.

ARI: You know, when you start to think about how much organizational energy that saves, it's a lot.

YANIK: And then, any tips on if we were going to write out our vision tonight, tomorrow, this weekend, and then bringing it to our team and saying OK let's go implement?

ARI: Yeah, well, in the beginning, like you said, we write the draft down, then you bring it to them as a draft and get their input because it doesn't mean you have to drop everything they don't like. But it's just good to find out while it's a draft sort of how people are going to feel about it. And again, to your point, the more people contribute and the more we make changes based on their input, the more likely it is that they're going to get on board and support it. But yeah, at some point you start going and the going part is the strategic planning which, again, everybody is already doing that, it's just that this is actually knowing where you're going to end up.

You know, the thing of doing with strategic planning without a clear vision of what success looks like, you know, in my mind is sort of like you're pulling up to an intersection, roll down the window, yell over to some guy walking down the block and say, "Hey, sir, should I turn left or right?" and we all know what he's going to say, which is, "Well, where are you going?" and you go, "Well, I don't really know, you know. What are the statistics more people turn left here or right here? And then actually I'm more interested in how your forecast are going to be turning three years from now so I can be ahead of the curve." See this is the curve.

You and I have a vision right here, we decide what the curve is, you know, we're going where we want to go, not where everybody else thinks we should go, and it's a very hard living from the outside in because it's hard running a business. Everybody who listens to the show knows that, and for me it keeps my energy way higher, and that's really a big piece of this is that people feel better about their work and they're more inspired to go after greatness and they start to do more and more of the little things that really make the business run every day and more effectively.

YANIK: Yeah, and you guys have been a case study in that for sure. You know, one thing that I want to mention or have you mention, how you see it all fitting together. You have a great diagram of the vision and then how it cascades down to culture and the training. Can you mention that for a minute?

ARI: Yeah, sure. It's a chart obviously. I can't paint the picture in an interview, but it's in the book, and my email is also at zingermans.com, we can get you a copy if you don't want to buy the book.

YANIK: Don't be a cheapskate, buy the book!

ARI: OK, buy the book. But anyway, it's a chart that we came up with in the mid-'90s. Maggie Bayless was one of the managing partners in ZingTrain— actually, she went back to school and got her MBA in Michigan. Her real passion is training, so in the same way that I get going working with the food, she loves training. And she taught us a lot of stuff which in hindsight of course it's ABC to the training world in many ways, but it served us enormously well.

And one of them was the obvious, that different people learn in different ways. And some people like visuals, and so we spent a good year, again, me, her, Paul, and whoever else sort of constructing this visual construct of how the organization works. And like you said, it's got the vision in it, mission statement. We measure on three bottom lines here, and we've been doing that for 15 years: food, quality service, quality and finance, are all bottom line. It's just for us and it talks about the culture, our guiding principles, our values, and then the systems that we use, and it's sort of all woven into that one little chart.

Well, I'll tell you, we really do use it in everything. The interesting thing is how much the employees all use it. So I got files on the computer just full of stories that people who work here have shared about how they use visioning and how much it's changed their whole approach. You know, most people are trained to find what's wrong. They're trained to find what's wrong with you and I as leaders. They're going to find what's wrong with the organization. They're going to find what's wrong with the customers.

They're going to find what's wrong with your life, and it's not like those things aren't wrong, but this is all about getting them to think positively. And so it does so much to just sort of get rid of the victim mindset that is so prevalent, I think, in society, because everybody here knows: Write a vision. So as soon as somebody starts complaining, somebody else goes, "Go ahead, write a vision, man, keep going." They all get it. They're like, if you want something, say what you want and then start working on it. It doesn't mean that they can just have their way because people got to prove things, but the point is if you don't say what you want and just saying what's wrong, nobody wants to hear it anymore.

YANIK: Right.

ARI: And people use it in their personal finances, they use it in their relationships. I got stories of people using it to plan their wedding. They used it to figure out how to get out of debt. It's really kind of wild in a good way. It's pretty amazing how much I think it really actually has impacted people's lives outside of the job.

Question-and-Answer Time

ADAM: Thanks for the wonderful insights, Ari. Quick question, I want to kind of ask about what Yanik had mentioned; the ability to say "No." How much of your vision statements have negative comments versus positive comments?

ARI: That's a good question. We try to pretty much keep it in the positive and it's always a way to flip the negative into a positive. And this is all about positive futuring, so it's really saying what you want and what's going to get you excited, as opposed to what you don't want.

ADAM: Gotcha. It seems that if you're able to say no to a lot of things—as you had mentioned, you're not going to go public. That really helps to define the culture. I have not read your vision statement, yet, but would you say what percent is clarifying the parts of where the company and your personal beliefs are?

ARI: I don't know, I never really, you know, placed it like that. I think really it just describes what our organization is going to be like, the new one in the year 2020. And it talks about making our world around us better. It talks about, again, this idea of having this community of businesses all located in the Ann Arbor area, each business with the managing partner or partners in it, each with its own specialty operating as one organization.

It talked about radically better food and service than what we have today. It talked about radically better finance, which really means for us a sustainable finance for ourselves as an organization, for the people in the organization, etc. It talks about being an educational destination. It talks about fun in the organization. It talks about opportunity and responsibility for everybody in the organization, etc., and it's just a picture of what it's going to be like. And to Yanik's point, there's a lot of descriptive stuff in there. It's not just sort of six bullet points.

ADAM: How far do you tend to drill down into these areas?

ARI: Well, there's no right or wrong answer. It should be enough detail that it means something, and so saying "We're the best," it doesn't really mean a lot. Saying that Yanik Silver came to visit and couldn't stop talking about how amazing our company was, I mean, those are like small, anecdotal things that actually mean something. And I don't know what those things are for you, but saying we're going to grow rapidly, well, what does that mean? Five percent, 10 percent, 20 percent, 40 percent? One person's rapid is another one's slow. But it's deciding what the growth is that you want, not the growth that just comes, and trying to get as big as you can as fast as you can is not a vision, it's reactive.

JOYCE: How do you tell people not to get discouraged? Because people could have vision but when there are obstacles they can give up.

ARI: Well, I don't tell them not to get discouraged. I think that you should know that you're going to get discouraged. It's just what to do when you are discouraged. I think you got to get around good people because this is the whole thing of positive stuff, right? It's that if you are around people that are negative a lot, it's only a matter of time before they are going to get negative about you. You know—and I don't mean pie-in-the-sky—it's just you want to be around people who are going to pull through, and it's no different than a sports team or whatever.

There's no championship team that en route to the championship hasn't had dark days or bad games or was down 22 halfway through the second quarter, but they can look back on how they turned it around. Rosabeth Moss

Kanter has a book out called *Confidence*, which I recommend highly, which is a lot about winning teams and losing teams. But I think that having the vision out there written down for me, you know, would be embarrassing not to get there.

GONZALES: My question is, me being a young entrepreneur and I like to do a lot of things on my own, but do you find it more successful if you work with a partner or carrying your vision out on your own?

ARI: You know, honestly, that's part of your vision, because having worked with partners for

> ## Maverick Resource
>
> Pick up a copy of Ari's book, *A Lapsed Anarchist's Approach to Building a Great Business*. It's available at zingtrain.com. I've read it through now, marked it up heavily, and totally love the book.

a long time, I'm a big believer, but it does slow you down. The truth is, you don't really get your own way all the time, anyway. But even more obviously, that you don't get your own way all the time and you got to really learn collaboration and negotiation and dialogue. But at the same time I got a lot of friends who are doing it on their own. It's a lonely way to go.

AN EXEMPLARY VISION

OK. Now I want to show you a few pages of our own Painted Pictures and vision for the group of Maverick companies (Figure 2.1, beginning on page 44, shows the cover page and a few of the interior pages) so you can see exactly what visioning looks like. You can download the whole thing in color at www.MaverickBusinessAdventures.com/vision.

FIGURE 2.1 Painted Maverick Business Lifestyle group's 2012 painted picture example

Maverick Core:

Maverick companies embody the internal and external philosophy of 'Make More Money, Have More Fun, and Give More'. Business bliss and balance are found where all 3 connect.

Maverick DNA:

1. **A Little Bit Quirky, a Little Bit Rock n' Roll** - not taking ourselves too seriously while having something pretty damn frickin' cool going on!

2. **C'mon Baby Light My Fire** - creating the spark & connection for successful entrepreneurs.

3. **But Wait, There's More...** Obviously taken from a typical infomercial line, this is a driving goal of creating surprise, delight and astonishment beyond expectations.

4. **Ripple** – Maverick is not just a pebble thrown in a pond, but a boulder. We create massive impact with our charitable and philanthropic innovation, entrepreneurship and giving forward.

5. **Banish the Ordinary.** Why have an ordinary life or create an ordinary business? You make the rules and that's what we're all about.

Surrounding the Maverick core is the '**Entrepreneurial Success Continuum**'. Many entrepreneurs typically begin with *Start-Up*, move into the *Growth* phase, and then evolve into the *Legacy* phase, where they want to give. Maverick Business Lifestyle is involved in each aspect of an entrepreneur's development beginning with the *Start-Up Phase*...

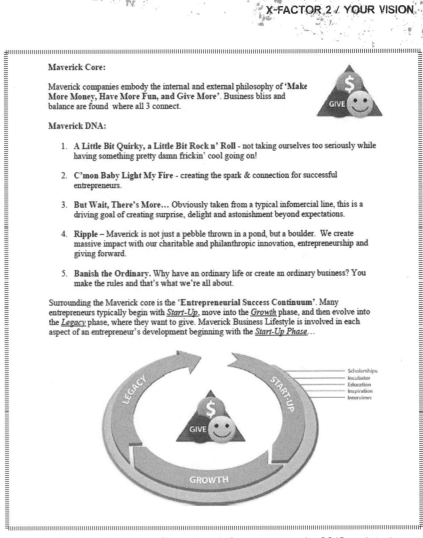

FIGURE 2.1 Painted Maverick Business Lifestyle group's 2012 painted picture example, continued

Funding is provided by a portion of each sale from the Maverick brand. Each product sold is tied into a result-oriented, specific charitable transaction inspired by Tom's shoes; where one pair of shoes creates a donation of one pair of shoes in a 3rd world country. (i.e. 1 Maverick UpStart Camp scholarship for each Maverick Millionaire™ Retreat ticket sold.) Funding is also generated from our unique and fun fundraising adventures. The foundation runs the Maverick1Million.ORG and disburses funds to other entrepreneurial charities we work with such as Village Enterprise Fund, Kiva.org and Virgin Unite.

Maverick Brand - inspires a passionate level of belonging and affinity among entrepreneurial members at all income levels. *Astonishment Architecture*™ is part of the brand experience where each member touch point is specifically designed to astonish, wow or over-deliver on expectations. Maverick members create their own language and rituals. The right companies consistently approach us to license the Maverick brand for products ranging from tools like laptops and smart phones to entrepreneurial luxuries such as private jet sharing cards. Due to the high affinity, we produce uniquely branded apparel and consumables in limited editions to allow entrepreneurs to be identified with the Maverick Business Lifestyle in their day-to-day lives.

Partnerships - Maverick only partners with the top-level brands that enhance value for members. For example, a co-branded Maverick VISA card allows cardholders to qualify for Maverick experiences. VISA also provides unique access for Maverick members to events it sponsors like the World Cup and Olympics. Partnerships are not just a banner inside the learning center but are truly integrated across all aspects of Growth, Start-up and Legacy.

Press – Maverick Business Lifestyle's unique activities, adventures, high-impact training and young entrepreneur focus continue to gain numerous mentions in the top business, lifestyle and travel publications, even landing the front cover of INC & Fast Company.

Team: The Maverick Business Lifestyle team is a results-based virtual team that thrives in a culture of autonomy, meaning and tons of fun! There are no assigned hours or office to report to. Each member develops and contributes their Unique Ability. Unique ability is based on Dan Sullivan's concept of identifying your best habits with continual improvement, passion and energy from performing that activity. Team members are selected for their DNA culture match first and skill set second. We use Kolbe testing to allow team members to work in their natural connotative flow. Every six months team members are rewarded with unique perks such as time off & the funding to accomplish an item on their 'Ultimate Big Life List' as well as a charitable contribution to a cause of their choice.

FIGURE 2.1 Painted Maverick Business Lifestyle group's 2012 painted picture example, continued

X-Factor 3

HIGH MARGINS AND PREMIUM PRICES

WHY DON'T THEY SELL FERRARIS AT KMART?

You have to charge a premium price so you can provide an extraordinary experience and value. People are just banging their heads against the wall trying to undercut their competitors. I think that's totally wrong!

About two years ago, I conducted a $10,000-per-person workshop on "How to Sell Super-High-Priced Information Products and Services" (www.InfoPlayersWorkshop.com), and I'll share a few insights here.

If you boil down my biggest profit windfalls in my business (and those of the most astute marketers I observe), it comes down to selling premium products and services at premium prices. That's how my business has leapfrogged from five figures to six figures to seven figures, and now multiple seven-figure gigs a year!

Personally, I've sold everything from $5,000 workshops to $14,500 "Apprentice Programs" to $20,000 "MasterMind" groups, and even a $40,000-per-year program for cosmetic surgeons.

Let's take a few numbers.

Perhaps you want to make an extra million this year; then you'd have to sell 20,000 copies of your doohickey at $50. Or it could be 2,000 copies at $500. Or, better still, 200 copies at $5,000. It's a lot easier dealing with 200 customers than 20,000. Think of all the customer service and infrastructure, etc.

SIX REASONS WHY YOU SHOULD CHARGE PREMIUM PRICES FOR YOUR PRODUCT OR SERVICE

Once again, before we get into the "how" let's discuss the "why."

Reason 1. More Profits

OK, no surprise here. When you sell for higher prices, you make more profits. Very few companies have been able to sustain a "low-price" position in the marketplace. Sears couldn't. Kmart couldn't. And now it remains to be seen what Walmart does with that position. (Actually if you study Walmart, you'll notice they are bringing in some significantly high-priced, high-margin products.)

Reason 2. Better Customers

Price qualifies your customers more than you might realize. The ones that pay $7 for an ebook are going to be the ones who whine and complain the most! They'll tax and strain your customer support team. But in comparison, the customers who spend significant amounts of money are surprisingly easier to deal with and less demanding.

Think about the last time you gave free advice to someone, what happened? That's right. Nothing. But if you had made them pay you for consulting, they would have taken it to heart.

Reason 3. The Psychology of Pricing Works in Your Favor

This is a big one! We've always been taught, "You get what you pay for." It's not uncommon for a prospective customer to discount a product or offering because it's "too cheap." If the price is not in line with what it should be, you'd think there is something wrong.

Reason 4. You Can Deliver More Value

Ultimately the value you provide will dictate the profits you receive from your customers. Increase the value and your revenues go up. By selling high-profit products with high margins, you have lots more wiggle room to deliver sensational value. You can really wow your customers and buyers. Not only can you throw in high-value extras, but you can afford to deliver truly unique, unadvertised, bonuses and follow-ups.

Reason 5. Some Buyers Will NOT Buy Low-Priced Items

It sounds crazy, but some customers are only premium buyers. If you gave them a discount, it would actually decrease the response. Plus, some customers are only comfortable buying in the high-end range. I was shocked when I discovered this with my first high-priced offering. My Apprentice program was $14,500, and at the time this was head and shoulders above any other marketer.

I thought my best prospects for this program would be customers who had already bought from me and were happy. Surprisingly, about half of the people in this program had NEVER bought anything from me before. Their comfort level was secured by a premium offer.

Reason 6. You Will OWN the Marketplace

I think this is the biggest reason of all.

This means you can afford to pay more to acquire a customer. This is huge! If I'm in the same marketplace and I'm competing against someone who only has a $100 product at the end of their funnel, and I have a $10,000 offering, there's going to be almost no contest. I can spend more on pay-per-click internet ads, more on traditional advertising, more on affiliate pay-outs, more on offline follow-up, more on testing unusual advertising places, etc.

And I can make bad results work for me. If I'm direct mailing for a high-priced product, I only need a fraction of a fraction of a fraction of the response for a low-priced product to make me money.

Fact is, the business owner who can spend the most to acquire a customer will WIN.

Period. End of story.

Most people are undercharging for what they provide. My rule of thumb, and one of my values I look at every morning in my planners, says, "I get rich by enriching others 10x—100x what they pay me in return."

That's a big deal for me. If you pay me $1,000 for a product, I want to make sure it delivers you $10,000 in value. I suggest you consider something similar. If your product isn't good enough for you to raise your price on it, make it better!

THREE STEPS TO ENSURE YOUR PRODUCT OR OFFERING HAS HIGH PERCEIVED VALUE

Charging a premium needn't make you nervous about pricing yourself out of the market. The first step at the "how" to double or triple your price is to start brainstorming the value you provide.

Step 1. Brainstorming Additional Value

Either find a trusted advisor, work with your team (if you have one), or just grab a blank, yellow legal pad and start coming up with answers. It doesn't matter how crazy they are. Just write them all down. In fact, the rules of brainstorming should be used:

Rule 1. No criticism allowed (turn off your left brain).
Rule 2. The wilder the better; everything's possible.
Rule 3. Quantity of ideas

Rule 4. Jump off and "plus" other ideas. (In other words work like improv actors would by saying "Yes, and . . ." to continue the thought and idea to make it even better.)

You want to start with a blank slate and just contemplate "blue sky" questions like these:

- ▶ "How can I provide 10 to 100 times the value my customers expect?"
- ▶ "What can I do that will absolutely amaze them?"
- ▶ "How can I get my customers the result they want on a silver platter?"
- ▶ "How can I 'do it for them'?"

Step 2. Check Your Thinking

Setting higher prices begins inside your head. People are usually too slow to raise prices, and it's more about confidence and self-image than the actual value delivered. Get Maxwell Maltz's book, *Psycho Cybernetics*, and consider your self-image. We all have self-images in every single area of our life, and if you are not charging a premium, it's usually more to do with what's in between your ears than the actual marketplace. Which brings me to my next point: Never allow your competition to set your prices. Just because someone else charges x dollars, that does not mean you have to charge similar prices. There will always be a very profitable spot for businesses at the premium scale who deliver what's perceived as exceptional products and value.

Step 3. Targeting the Right Marketplace

Another mistake I see a lot is going after markets that cannot afford to pay premium prices. There's no reason you cannot have another division of your business go after customers who have already shown they will pay premium prices for products/services. For example, I have a giclée of a painting by Thomas Arvid in our dining room at home. I believe we paid between $2,500 and $3,000 for this work. Now, in case you are unfamiliar with the term, a giclée is really just a fancy print, this one being on canvas. I can most certainly assure you there is a high margin in this piece.

Why would I and many others pay such a premium for it? Well, the artist's originals go for $25,000 or more now (if you can even get them), and he chose a subject that buyers would pay a premium for—high-end wines. Also, it's a limited edition piece (something we'll discuss in greater detail shortly). Arvid only specializes in hyper-realistic wine paintings. They are absolutely beautiful, and the first time I saw his work in Carmel, California, I was blown away. (You can see for yourself at www.arvid.com.) Arvid paints high-end wines like Opus One, Silver Oak, Caymus, etc.

And the people who are passionate about these high-end wines will pay a premium for wonderful art. He stumbled onto this by accident when he started painting and found that a red wine painting was snapped up immediately. Very astutely, Arvid learned more about wine and which ones to paint so that customers would open up their wallets.

And the final aspects of creating a high-priced offer are the psychological ones.

We've talked about the psychology of scarcity previously. Human beings have been hard-wired to want what is going away. Many more people are motivated by the thought of potential loss than potential gain. You see this used all the time in marketing, and it works IF there is truth behind it or we perceive there to be truth behind it. Here's one example from a company I buy a lot of wine from, that really illustrates this point (combined with "reason why"). See Figure 3.1.

If you have trouble reading the text in the email, here's the main part (emphasis in italic is my own):

WINE ALERT: As you probably read in the news, our friends at Silver Oak experienced a terrible fire at their winery earlier this year. At that time, there were *rumors that they had lost most of their past and current vintages*. Hence, *the winery ceased new sales*

FIGURE 3.1 Marketing that taps the psychology of exclusivity
Reprinted with permission of Porthos.com ©2009. All rights reserved.

of their prized Silver Oak 2001 Alexander Valley Cabernet—
Robert Parker's highest rated Silver Oak since renowned 1997
vintage—to the great disappointment of thirsty collectors across
America who have made this wine the #1 selling Collector
Cabernet. However, today the big news is our friends at Silver
Oak just found 15 more cases of this wine + several BIG bottles
including an *extremely rare* 6L quadruple magnum (details
below) safely tucked away in their private cellar and have made
an exclusive offer to Porthos Insiders on a "first come, first sell"

basis. *These are the last cases and only big bottles of this prized vintage that will ever be available for sale so don't miss this insiders-only offer!*

In case you are wondering which one I bought, it was the 6L quadruple magnum (that's equivalent to 8 regular bottles). I really like Silver Oak anyway, so I wouldn't have bought this just because it was so scarce (or at least I tell myself that). I'm planning on popping this bad boy for some big celebration.

With this information, the only thing stopping you from raising your price is yourself. But if you want to just try it out, you can always start small by adding a "Deluxe" or "Gold" version of your existing product or service and see what happens. I think you'll be pleasantly surprised, by adding some of these elements to your marketing, how you can easily double or triple your prices and still provide an incredible value.

X-Factor 4

GET IT OUT THE DOOR

IT'LL NEVER BE PERFECT—DEAL WITH IT

It's too easy to wait until you have the perfect product or service—but when is that, exactly?

Get your idea out there as fast as possible, even if it's not quite ready, by setting must-hit deadlines. Let the market tell you if you have a winner or not. If not, move on and fail forward fast! If it's got potential, then you can make it better.

The sooner you get your product out the door, the quicker you'll be able to start getting marketplace feedback for X-Factors 5 and 6.

I always wait until the last-minute to get things done. I remember for a recent Maverick experience to Iceland, I didn't even look at my packing list until two days before I was leaving, only to realize I needed waterproof hiking boots for the glaciers, long Under Armor® pants for SCUBA, etc. Missy wanted me to get some booster shots at the doc, and she wanted to buy a car—all before I left. Sheesh!

If you stop and think about this, the deadline of my impending trip made these must-happen events. This creates a true deadline, and I believe that's the secret of getting things done in many cases. There's been numerous times in my business I've artificially created that "deadline" to get me moving.

In 1998, my very first info product selling to dermatologists helping them attract more cosmetic patients was only created because I set up a deadline for myself. I was working for my Dad at the time, selling medical equipment, and on the side, I was going to give this info marketing a try. I ran a small classified ad in *Dermatologic Surgery* magazine and got ten leads. I had the sales letter all ready and sent it off to them.

Then I waited and watched the fax machine at my Dad's office . . .

And I waited . . .

And waited . . .

I sent a second notice and finally a third notice tied to an impending deadline for the doctors to get several bonuses. On that day of the deadline, I got a fax coming through with an order for $900. YES!! I was so incredibly excited, but after I peeled myself off the ceiling, I realized I did not have the course ready. I had an outline that I used when I wrote the sales letter, but really not much else. So I sent a note to my first order (I still remember his name) and told him the manual was being republished and would be available in 30 days. And I mentioned I wouldn't charge his card until it shipped. So you better believe I busted my ass till 3 A.M. or 4 A.M. most nights getting the manual done in that deadline period. But the deadline and that unprocessed order gave me incentive to get it finished and started me on the path to making millions selling information.

Funny how deadlines can do that for you.

I've used this same thing repeatedly. When I did my very first live event—my 30th Birthday Bash—I just set the date and figured it would all fall into place. I didn't have speakers, a venue, etc. Nothing but an idea of trying to get 500 people there. We ended up with 562.

When I first launched Maverick Business Adventures®, I decided the first trip would be January 2008, and I would figure out the rest as we went along. The deadlines work! And you can make this concept work for you on a small scale, too. I've done this when procrastinating on auto-responder messages. I would stick up an opt-in box offering up a multipart course (i.e., a weeklong course or something like that). Then, once I started getting people to subscribe, I was obligated to finish up the next auto-responder message before the week was up.

GET PAID BEFORE YOU CREATE JUST ABOUT ANYTHING

I'm a big fan of starting small and testing your idea before blowing eight months working on something and tens of thousands of dollars to discover nobody frickin' gives a damn! Aaack!

Two of the coolest sites I've seen in a while are IndieGoGo.com and KickStarter.com

If you've got some sort of project in mind, and it has legs, you can check the pulse of the market at these two spots first. It's pretty easy to get going with this. You just need to:

▸ Work on explaining the project in print or, ideally, in a video
▸ Come up with the dollar amount you want to raise
▸ Pick a date for the deadline to raise funds
▸ Come up with cool and unique gifts to reward the backers (i.e., autographed copy of your work, unique access, acknowledgment somewhere special, etc.)

That's about it. If the project gets funded, you receive the dough, less the transaction fees. If you don't raise the amount, all the money is refunded to the supporters.

So let's take a peek at a successful recent project (see Figure 4.1, page 58).

Here's one that as of this writing has ended up raising more than $24,600 for a new product. Pretty sweet. You can see the campaign here: www.indiegogo.com/Mobile-Video-Accessory.

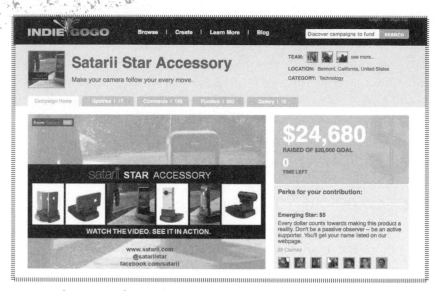

FIGURE 4.1 A successful capital-raising campaign on Indiegogo.com
Reprinted with permission of Indiegogo ©2011. All rights reserved.

This is a cool gadget to allow your camera to automatically follow you. It's a pretty interesting invention, but what's even more interesting to me is the fact the marketplace actually paid for it in advance. Most people who have ideas will spend a ton of money and time hoping they can sell—but using one of the crowd funding sites you can figure it out pretty quickly.

They've done a couple really smart things. They've done a good job creating perks that make you feel like you are an insider and someone important to creating (or designing) this product. See Figure 4.2.

Another smart technique is having funding options at higher prices, which always helps you get to your goal quicker. See Figure 4.3 on page 60.

There are lots of book authors, printmakers, artists, musicians, etc., who have embraced these sites and others like it for this unique "crowd-funded patron" model.

The other thing I really love about this model is the kind of stories it creates from the first backers of any project. I'm always talking about how to create stories for your marketing message to get passed along,

Star: $25

Make an impact! You'll get listed as a supporter, be placed on a list for an opportunity to be one of the first to buy the retail product at a discount, and get a Satarii t-shirt (design TBD with the help of supporters). (US shipping included)

168 Claimed

Rock Star: $75

Want to influence our design? You'll get listed as a supporter, be placed on list to be one of the first to buy the retail product at discount, get a t-shirt, and an opportunity to meet with Satarii in a focus group environment to check out the system and give direct feedback. (US shipping included)

9 Claimed   (Sold Out!)

FIGURE 4.2 Special perks create more buy-ins

and by having your customers feel like they are on the inside and truly part of the startup like this creates that. Won't they talk about it? Absolutely! (That hits on another X-Factor upcoming.)

Super Star: $200

Be the first to use it! You'll get listed as a supporter, a t-shirt, and you are pre-ordering one of our integrated tracking systems (standard color). (US shipping included)

23 Claimed (Sold Out!)

Super Star Plus: $225

Want it for your pocket camera? You'll get listed as a supporter, a t-shirt, you are pre-ordering an Integrated System (standard colors), and you get our tripod mount accessory. (US shipping included)

22 Claimed (Sold Out!)

Nova: $350

Something extra special. You'll get listed as a supporter and you are pre-ordering one of our integrated tracking systems (limited edition colors), and you become a design adviser. (US shipping included)

13 Claimed (Sold Out!)

FIGURE 4.3 Higher levels of creative perks allows you to raise more funds quickly

The other thing is you don't have to just use one of these platforms. You can always go direct to your customers or list with a "pre-creation" offer. I did this with an e-book I had about 75 percent done, all about broadcast faxing (Note: This was released when broadcast faxing was legal.) Getting the orders coming in helped motivate me to finish it.

Here's the email I used to sell this:

Special Prepublication Announcement

Dear <firstname>,

Would you like to know how I spent $418 and brought in $35,717.00 in sales, practically overnight?

Are you interested in how you can create instant sales, generate hot leads and make immediate profits without ever leaving your desk?

If so, then listen up . . .

Because you'll want to know about a new manual I'm just finishing called *How to Make Instant Sales and Immediate Profits with Cheap Broadcast Faxes*.

Inside I give away all my trade secrets I've used to achieve massive returns of 15 to 1 (or more). Fact is, most marketing pros are ecstatic if their ad pays for itself so a 1500 percent ROI is tremendous!

Plus, inside I've even included a whole section of my actual fax ads where I explain in step-by-step detail how I created these winners so you can simply turn around and do the exact same thing!

But now here's the best part—for a limited time, I'm making a special pre-publication deal where you can save $50.00 off the regular price. Not only that, but you also get $400.00 in free bonuses and everything comes with my 100% unconditional, one-year guarantee. So you really can't lose!

Do yourself a favor and check out the full story at:

⇒ http://Site

Take care,

Yanik Silver

P.S. Don't worry, your credit card will not be charged or your check will not be cashed until the manual is ready to be delivered.

For this chapter on "Getting it out the door," I asked my Down Under friend, Ed Dale, of www.EdDale.co, to give his riff on this (and another big reason I like seeing if we can get some orders in the door early.)

On Burning the Ships–Maverick Wisdom, Courtesy of Ed Dale

One of the great romantic notions of striking out and starting your own business is the classic "burn the ship" story.

Apparently (and there is some dispute about this) when Spanish conquistador Hernando Cortez landed in Mexico, one of his first orders to his men was to burn the ships. Cortez was committed to his mission and did not want to allow himself or his men the option of going back to Spain. By removing this option, Cortez and his men were forced to focus on how they could make the mission successful.

I'm surprised at the number of people who start an online business and take the same approach. I'm even more surprised that right-thinking people would recommend this!

How does this apply to starting an online business?

Budding full-time business builders build up a bank of three months, six months, 12 months, and plan to dedicate themselves to starting an online business from scratch. This next sentence is not going to make me popular: It never works.

OK, I've never seen it work. I'm sure you can point me to a dozen examples of where someone has metaphorically "burned the ships" and started a new life. In six years of doing the 30-day challenge, and seeing thousands of online businesses start, I've never seen it work once.

After speaking to many victims, I have a theory why it doesn't work.

Before I look at the theory, I have reviewed many examples of successful online businesses. Guess what: In every case the person who created the successful

On Burning the Ships, continued

online business was working on something else (and being paid!) when they came up with the online business idea.

Steve Jobs was working at Atari, Woz [Steve Wozniak, Jobs' partner], an engineer at Hewlett-Packard. The founders of YouTube were working at PayPal. Dell was created as a sideline in a college dorm room.

It dawned on me: All these ideas, which eventually became new businesses, were generated while the person was doing something else.

What about people who open cafes? Don't they "burn the ships"? I would argue no. The idea to start a cafe, the saving up and getting of loans, and all the other horror involved in opening a cafe are done while doing something else. A person with no income cannot suddenly decide tomorrow to open a cafe.

I have racked my brain to come up with one successful online business that has started from a "burn the ships" scenario.

I can think of none.

Back to my theory.

To explain my pop theory, I have to reach back to my year eight social sciences class and discuss (and without a doubt, butcher) the concept of Maslow's hierarchy of needs.

Say what?

http://en.wikipedia.org/wiki/Maslow%27s_hierarchy_of_needs

Wikipedia reads:

> Maslow's hierarchy of needs is often portrayed in the shape of a pyramid, with the largest and most fundamental levels of needs at the bottom, and the need for self-actualization at the top.

On Burning the Ships, continued

> The most fundamental and basic four layers of the pyramid contain what Maslow called "deficiency needs" or "d-needs": esteem, friendship and love, security, and physical needs. With the exception of the most fundamental (physiological) needs, if these "deficiency needs" are not met, the body gives no physical indication but the individual feels anxious and tense. Maslow's theory suggests that the most basic level of needs must be met before the individual will strongly desire (or focus motivation upon) the secondary or higher level needs. [Like starting a business.]

Stay with me, I'll bring this all home. Let me explain how the average "burn the ships" scenario goes. Sadly, I have seen this too many times.

Jane Smith does a brilliant job, and saves up a bank of six months' worth of food, rent, and utility bills. She's been dreaming of the day she can finally chuck everything and focus solely on an online business. Once she's free of working "for the man" she can finally create an online business; to work on the business full time, she is sure, is the missing link.

Mistake 1: No Idea, No Research, No Market

The first two months of this ambitious "burn the ships" project are fantastic. Jane watches all the webinars, clears Google reader every day, finally gets to study all of the courses sitting on the shelf. It's a brilliant time.

For some reason, one thing doesn't happen: a massive amount of testing. There is a reveling in the new-found freedom and lifestyle of being a professional online marketer, but very little testing.

The first signs of trouble typically happen just before the halfway mark. Jane can't believe it was just eight weeks ago when she stuck it to the man quitting her job. She only has four months to go. It's time to buckle down, listen to Ed's "Going Pro" speech and really starting to take action. I better get the team member Ed is always rabbiting on about.

On Burning the Ships, continued

Mistake 2: Getting Your First Full-Time Team Member Takes Two Months

While Jane goes through the process of trying to find a team member, she starts to research phrases and markets. She's still calm and purpose-driven at this point. This is the high point of productivity in the "burning ships" project.

Hitting the halfway mark always causes a reflective moment. All of a sudden, from out of the blue, there are less days of this ambitious project than what has already been. The majority of this crazy adventure is already over! We are on the downhill slope. This is where things really go Jersey Shore.

Hail Mary

Time at this point seems to go so fast. Outsourcers don't work out, things go wrong, the wheels start to fall off the wagon.

Most crucially, the money is running out and those very real-world obligations are starting to invade in your subconscious and conscience. These are dark days. It's not pretty.

It's at this point, "burn the ships" turns into something far worse. We see another failed approach—the Hail Mary.

Jane gets increasingly desperate to make something happen. She tries to force the result. She tests phrases that previously wouldn't have cut the mustard. She realizes she's dropped off on the consistency backlinking requires, tried to do it herself because she doesn't have the time or the money to hire a team member. It becomes a vicious spiral. Sloppy research, sloppy backlinking, reaching for ideas and inspiration, cursing every person and idea leading her down this path.

Online marketing doesn't work. It's all a scam.

On Burning the Ships, continued

At this point, Jane is joined by another group of people we often see at the challenge, the "got 30 days until declared bankrupt" crowd. Please, read this carefully, I have enormous sympathy for people in this situation. It's heartbreaking.

At this point people need a lottery win. It's just not going to happen.

I've never seen a Hail Mary work. I've never seen a "burn the ships" project work.

If you think you can start any new endeavour with the threat of losing your house over your head, you can. According to Maslow, it's just not going to work.

I concur, I've NEVER seen it work.

Unless you've got the basics of food and shelter sorted and a break from the relentless calls of the credit card companies that gave you the easy credit in the first place, you're not in any state to start a business.

Sorry. That's just the way it is.

This is why those last couple of months in "burn the ships" projects are so dreadful. Heart-rendingly horrific. You may not be losing your house, but subconsciously, you're having exactly the same battle.

There is a massive difference between watching an ever-dwindling bank slowly go down and being safe in the knowledge enough income to eat and sleep is coming in each month. The path to success in an online business is paved by continuously doing the processes required to conduct an online business.

There's no gold medal without daily intensive training.

There's no online business without proper market research, implementation of traffic strategies and the proper use of conversion techniques.

On Burning the Ships, continued

These are not things to be rushed. The best ideas and the best results always come from working a process. The best headlines always come after you've written the bulk of the sales copy. The best arcs and storylines come from when you're neck-deep in writing the story (remind me to tell you about Stephen King's *On Writing* some time).

Just as the gold medal only comes from constant training, a successful business comes from constant work.

There is no inspiration, no golden ticket, no "Road to Damascus" moment.

There are certainly no Hail Marys.

Fortunately for you (and Jane), there's an alternative.

One of the big tenets I work on getting startups to think about is immediately getting marketplace feedback from potential users. While I'm not a huge fan of surveys (since people are not plunking down money), I do believe they have their place. One of the best uses of a survey integrated into a "coming soon" sort of release was a site I just saw.

Clutch is an iPhone app to help you in the event you lose your wallet (www.ItsClutch.com). Their "coming soon" page shows a few screenshots of how the app works and then proceeds to ask you for a survey response.

I like the fact they are capturing email addresses of interested prospects.

There are small commitment/consistency instances that help the potential of people actually buying this app once it's available. I don't know if the designers of Clutch are aware of the psychology of this

Maverick Resource

Another tool you might consider is www.LaunchRock.com. They provide an easy-to-use page builder that helps users virally spread the word about your new startup.

or not, but taking a page out of one of my favorite books, Robert Cialdini's *Influence: The Psychology of Persuasion*, they are getting small commitments (i.e., "I'd love to use this app!"), which will turn into a much higher percentage of people than normal buying that app if they've checked that box.

This is a cool example that's easy to implement for your next idea that you put up online.

HOW TO COME UP WITH A POWERFUL NAME FOR A NEW PRODUCT OR SERVICE

If we're going to get something out in the marketplace we need a name, right?

As Shakespeare said, "What's in a name? That which we call a rose by any other name would smell as sweet."

Bzzzzzz! Wrong!

I think one of the most overlooked aspects in marketing is naming a product or service. There's a lot to be said for coming up with the right name that helps propel your business forward instead of slogging along. And when I talk about new names here, keep in mind this applies to domain names and titles equally.

I mean think about it. In Hollywood, actors have known this since the start. Do you know who Marion Morrisson was? Nope? That's John Wayne's real name. He adopted a stage name because Marion doesn't exactly conjure up a tough-guy image. Norma Jeane Baker changed her name to conjure up a more glamorous Marilyn Monroe.

Here Are a Few More Examples

Ever heard of a Patagonian tooth fish? Sounds delicious, right? Not quite. But when they went with "Chilean sea bass," sales soared. Or how about the "Chinese gooseberry"—wouldn't you like to have that for a snack? No? Oh, OK, then, maybe "kiwi fruit" is a better name.

Names are quite powerful. Here's an historical example to prove my point. Originally, the United States was protected by its "Department of War" and later they changed it to a more peaceful-sounding "Department of Defense." One name brings up the notion the United States is constantly waging war on other countries, and without turning this into a political discussion, renaming it around defense is significantly more palatable, even if the function is the same.

Yes, there is a lot to a name, and I'll share with you what I consider before I give a name to a new product, service, or business. In a haphazard way, I've known how powerful names can be, starting when I was 16 years old and working with my father, selling medical equipment. We created a private-label X-ray film to be sold to our customers and my Dad tasked me to help with naming it. I came up with "Ultimate X-Ray Film" and it turned into a major bestseller.

Now, I got to thinking of names the other day, because Missy asked me to help her friend come up with a name for her new speaker management company. She was going to go with her last name, "Smith Management." Yuck! Boring!

I started thinking about what is the ultimate benefit a speaker would want. To me, it would be something about moving up to a higher level of fees, or being completely booked. So I came up with "Booked Solid Speaker Services." I thought that was way better and included a serious benefit. I guess not. She went with her generic last name for the company name. In my opinion—big mistake! There's no differentiation and no benefit.

Since I started really as a copywriter, words are incredibly important. Each one has a distinct difference. And if you get the name right, you get branding as a byproduct of powerful direct-response advertising for your product or service.

OK, so let me give you some of my ideas around naming:

A Little Alliteration Sounds Good

A name needs to sound good being said aloud. A lot of times I like alliteration like "Maverick Mastermind" with the 2 Ms. And the converse of this is you need to say your product name aloud and make sure it can't be screwed up on the radio or in conversation. Like, does "Computers for You" have a number "4" or just a letter "U" in it? I see this mistake a lot for domain names (by the way, all this advice holds true for domains).

Make Your Name Benefit-Oriented

Many times I like to use a name that has meaning to it. If you heard it, you'd know right away what it is. For my first "real" book *Moonlighting on the Internet* there's an instant benefit with the term "moonlighting"— it brings to mind a spare-time venture, perfect for my book, which is all about five ways to make a couple hundred dollars extra online.

Beware of the Web 2.0 Syndrome

For some reason after companies like Flickr or Del.icio.us got big, everybody wanted to create some sort of mildly dyslexic spelling for their company name that seemed cool. (I still don't know if I spell Flickr with an "er" or not. And I definitely have no idea how to spell Del.icio.us without looking it up.)

Beware Initials and Generics

Yes, some of the biggest companies like AT&T or IBM have gotten away with initials, but I wouldn't hold my breath thinking that'll work for you, too. And why would you? It's so damn boring. And along the same lines, don't use a generic name that doesn't mean Jack. You don't want your customer wondering, "Hmm . . . was I supposed to call Capital Paper Solutions or was it Senate Paper?"

Use Specifics

I like using numbers, days—specific time periods. My man, Tim Ferriss has made quite a splash with the title *4-Hour Work Week*. It's a pretty specific and compelling name for a lifestyle book. Other works that have sold well just from their specific titles include *8-Minute Abs* and 5-hour Energy. Personally, one of my bestselling ebooks has the title *33 Days to Online Profits*, once again, playing up the specifics.

Who Is Your Market?

The right kind of name will help you define who is attracted to your product or service. You might remember years back when Boston Chicken changed to Boston Market. I thought that was a bad idea because it was more generic; well, apparently others thought so, too, and it began losing sales. They changed the name back, but the damage was done already. Personally, I think more people should embrace tight markets with their name and not try to be everything to everybody.

Can You Trademark It?

This is an important consideration depending on how big you want to build your brand, but it's always worth checking the United States Patent and Trademark Office at uspto.gov or a new site called Trademarkia.com.

Let me share with you a few of the names I've created and give you the thinking behind them.

▶ *Instant Sales Letters*. Uses the benefit-driven name with the qualifier "Instant" added to the generic item I was selling. I'm a big believer in using qualifiers to help you get the domain you really want (i.e. instant, ultimate, magic, formula, system, etc. Names like Auto-responder Magic or UltimateDiscountDomains.com).

▶ *Underground® Online Seminar*. The term "underground" immediately brings to mind something secretive, so it was a perfect name for our seminar series around real-world people teaching about how they make millions online.

▶ *Internet Lifestyle*. I have liked the word "lifestyle" ever since I saw it featured in the book *Words That Work* by Frank Luntz. People can relate to a lifestyle because it's different for everybody, and the "Internet Lifestyle" embodies a lot of what I do.

▸ *Maverick Business Adventures®*. This was a name I'd worked on for a long time. Originally the name was going to be "Millionaire Business Adventures." I definitely didn't think it had the right ring to it so I kept brainstorming. I like the MBA initials as a play on Masters of Business Administration, and that's when the word "Maverick" stuck.

I've never really shown this before, but here's the logo for Millionaire Business Adventures. We were going to have different adventure activities on cuff links, but alas, I scrubbed it (see Figure 4.4). I think you'll agree Maverick Business Adventures was the better choice. The word "millionaire" comes loaded with some interesting connotations around who millionaires are. I think it's a good word for something that helps people achieve millionaire status. I know of an ongoing program called "Maui Millionaires" that has done really well. Though, for targeting a group of millionaires, I'm not so sure, even though the Bravo TV channel's *Millionaire Matchmaker* seems to defy this.

The ultimate test of your name is your marketplace, and you can always test different names using Google AdWords. That's what Tim Ferriss did for *4-Hour Work Week* before releasing it. And I did the same for *Moonlighting on the Internet* vs. *Moonlighting Online*.

Here's an interesting case study: www.marketingexperiments.com/ improving-website-conversion/domain-product-name-testing.html.

FIGURE 4.4 Power words

One product name (StockScreener 5.0) performed 17 percent better than the next best name. They tested 22 different names, and the worst performed at 300 percent worse just by changing the name. Makes you think and makes you consider that maybe you should not choose a domain name, product name, or service without running some Google AdWord tests.

And that's a perfect prelude to our next chapter.

X-Factor 5

TEST AND IMPROVE

HOW MUCH HIGHER IS HIGH?

The first time you put something out there it's probably going to be the worst it can be. Don't worry about it.

But by following X-Factor 5, you can get more leverage and output from the same input. Let me give you a few quick examples.

TEST DIFFERENT WORDING

If you have an ad that is working already, we want to see how much better we can do. Literally one word can make a difference. There have been tests where the ad's headline is "Put Music into Your Life" versus "Puts Music into Your Life." Adding the letter s has given a significant, double-digit change to the response.

Crazy, right?

We can keep testing one variable against another to see what we can do better because our ad, in this case, is going to cost us the same fixed amount regardless if we get five customers or ten customers, right? Or with the same amount of web traffic, we can start getting one more or two more people converting to buyers with no additional cost.

TEST DIFFERENT COLORS

Let me show you another intriguing one. My good friend Ryan Deiss has tested the background color of this and has seen a 31 percent increase in using robin's egg blue on some of his sites. Amazing!

Sometimes it can be the simplest things that have serious impact on your bottom line. See Figure 5.1.

FIGURE 5.1 Successful elements of advertising graphics

Internet marketing entrepreneur Jeff Mulligan and pilot Mark Robidoux co-founded in 2005 PilotWorkshops.com, an educational site for general aviation pilots. And they've used testing to make sure they're continually making their sales approach work even harder for them.

Maverick Resource

Ryan's DigitalMarketer.com testing laboratory is a great place for test results like that featured in Figure 5.1. Another one to check out is www.marketingexperiments. com/web-clinic/index.html.

CREATE A VARIETY OF BANNER ADS TO TEST

To promote their site, they use a multi-pronged marketing strategy that includes online banner ads. Rather than run one banner ad for a given product, the pair decided to implement an aggressive testing program to maximize results per dollar spent. This began a series of experiments where Mulligan and Robidoux brainstormed and created banners, and ran them on related websites.

Thanks to free tools like Google Analytics, virtually any company can do what the PilotWorkshops team did and track how many people each ad sends to their website. PilotWorkshops can also track which ad each customer replied to and bought from.

By correlating the responses with the ads, Mulligan was able to sift through the more than 20 different creative approaches they tested to find the top handful that significantly out-pulled the others. "Some of our best ads would perform four or five times better than the middle of the pack and ten times better than the worst. When you find a winner like that, it stretches your media-buying dollar four or five times further because you are getting so much better results with the same expenditure," explains Mulligan.

Another interesting fact was how often the team was surprised by the results. Mulligan explains, "Mark has been a pilot for years, and I've been writing headlines since 1986. You'd think we could reasonably predict which creative approaches might work best. But we learned that you never know what is going to work until you put it in front of people and measure their responses."

Now that the team has some proven, winning ads in its repertoire, they can more effectively test new media. Like any company that is spending money on advertising, PilotWorkshops is constantly approached by sales reps with new advertising outlets. They'll typically run a test using their best-performing ad. If that doesn't work, it's easy to call it quits and move on. On the other hand, when it does work, they have a new outlet where they can reach new customers. Knowing they are testing new media with a banner that is a proven performer removes a major variable in evaluating that website's advertising effectiveness.

Another important point is to rotate creative approaches. "You can't just find one winning ad and run it forever. It's different than print or broadcast. Online, you have to rotate creative much more frequently or it gets stale and click-through rates quickly plummet," says Mulligan.

I hope you're getting the picture on the different areas you can test to see how much better you can be doing. Here's one more I'll leave you with . . .

A WILD WAY TO INCREASE CONVERSION FROM 25 TO 40 PERCENT

I love this example because it shows you can take a pretty basic process (like a form), and add a little something to it, and you'll get a nice bump.

You remember using Mad Libs as a kid? You know, the game where you think of a type of animal or adjective or whatever, and it turns into a silly story. Well, I have to give credit to Luke Wroblewski's blog for ferreting out this cool example: www.lukew.com/ff/entry.asp?1007.

They point to a 25- to 40-percent bump by simply making the forms more conversational in nature. The form would use something like "I would like to use <Service> and I want my username to be _____ and I want my password to be _____."

Notice it encourages you in a conversational way to sign up and determine what you'd like your login and password to be. It works just like a standard form and just as you'd expect except for the way it's presented to you.

After seeing this, the team at Vast.com did an A/B split test with their traditional form and their newly revised, conversational one, and early results have bumped up responses by 25 to 40 percent

I wanted to see if they are still running these forms, and they are, and I still found it working for a car. Here's the form:

> Hello, my name is [first name] [last name] and I'm writing you today to learn more about the 2006 Acura MDX Touring listed for $24,995. I live in the [zip] area and I would like to hear back from you soon and learn more about this vehicle. Please call me at [my phone number] at your earliest convenience.

This is a huge bump in response!

X-Factor 6

LISTEN AND SHIFT

8-BALL SIDE POCKET AND OFF THE BANK

Let me start this chapter with a quick story.

To set the stage, January 1, 2000, I was in a one-bedroom apartment and was engaged to Missy. I didn't have a website and I had barely even started using email.

That same month was when I got an idea at 3 o'clock in the morning and woke Missy up to tell her about "Instant Sales Letters." (She wasn't happy!) And then I did what most people probably wouldn't: I hopped out of bed, registered the domain, and got to work on it. By February 2000, with about $1,500 invested, I made my first $29.95 sale. It was one of the most amazing feelings in the world to take an idea and have it turn into cash. And the sales kept coming: about $1,800 the first month, then $3,400, then approx. $7,800, and roughly $9,400 the fourth month out of the gate. I was on track to hit six figures with the InstantSalesLetters.com site, and that's when things really started exploding.

As people started hearing about my success, I was invited to speak at my first online marketing conference, and I started helping others take their interests, passions, hobbies and create their own "online oil wells."

THE UNUSUAL WAY TO STUMBLE ONTO SUCCESS

There's a profound theory, illustrated in Figure 6.1, from R. Buckminster Fuller that says your true success is found perpendicular along the path to your original, perceived goal. Instant Sales Letters is a perfect example, because my original goal was to sell it for $500,000 to Stamps. com or someone like that. But on my way to building up that site, I had so many people ask me how I started making money so quickly that I began teaching. And that teaching became part of my "accidental" success path opening up one door after another. I would never have got on that track unless I was moving toward the original goal. And it's the same thing today—the next chapter in my life is with the Maverick1000 network and Maverick Business Adventures®, which wouldn't have been formed without the contacts, connections, and success delivered from my internet business.

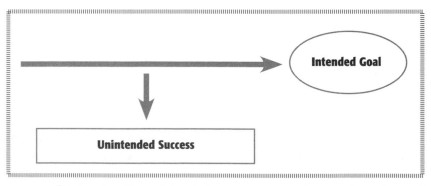

FIGURE 6.1 Don't miss the unintended success on your way to your goal!

Trust me, most businesses don't get it right the first time. That's OK. Your job is to listen closely to what your first customers love about what you are doing and see where you can deliver a bigger value for them there. There are lots of examples of companies that started as one thing and got their big breakthrough when they shifted.

UNINTENDED SUCCESS STORIES

First, there's the big daddy e-commerce site right now—Groupon.com. Groupon first started in 2006 as a company called ThePoint.com. It was a platform to mobilize people to band together across different causes or actions. But the thing that moved the needle was group buying, which spun off to make Groupon the fastest company to reach a billion dollars in valuation.

Or how about a group dating site that finds it's really a big hit in certain communities? At the end of 2008, Ignighter.com had 50,000 users in the United States. Not a big enough number to really get much traction. However, they were getting a lot of traffic from Singapore, Malaysia, India, and South Korea. Ignighter was gaining hundreds of users a day, mainly from New Delhi, Mumbai, Hyderabad, and Chennai. In January 2010, they made the decision to be strictly an Indian dating site. Now they have nearly two million users and are getting more than 7,000 signs-ups daily.

Your job as a Maverick entrepreneur is to figure out what in your business is starting to get traction and how you can make that a bigger focus. Many times it's something you least expect. It could be one single product or offering flying off the shelves. It could be a single feature in a piece of software you developed. You'll see it when you start looking for it.

X-Factor 7

CREATE ZEALOTS, SUPER FANS, AND ADVOCATES

I LOOOOVE YOU, MAN!

Let's face it: Companies that can harness the power of extremely loyal customers win! They get to spend less on advertising and marketing, their customers keep buying in droves, and they even love to evangelize and spread the merits of that product or service.

Sounds awesome, right?

There are some well-worn cult brand examples from big business, such as Harley-Davidson customers getting tattoos of the logo all over their bodies. I mean, if that's not a hard-core fan, I don't know what is. Or how about Apple customers waiting in line for days for the latest tech gizmo from their beloved manufacturer? (I haven't quite drunk the Kool-Aid, but I'm a Mac user and fan. I converted about two years ago and would never go back to a PC.)

Is there a way to engineer this? Yes and no.

FIGURE 7.1 Maverick members showing their passionate fan side before a World Cup match

Some of it will have to happen organically, but there is still a lot you can help foster. It's a combination of several factors.

STORIES SPREAD THE MESSAGE

For your message to get broadcast, it's important for consumers to be able to get it quickly and be able to connect.

We all have a "creation story," but few of us use them in our marketing. Think of it like a comic book character. If I asked you, "Who was bitten by a radioactive spider and started fighting crime to avenge his uncle's death?" You'd probably know this was Peter Parker, aka Spider Man. Or, "Who came from a dying planet and had super-human strength and abilities on our planet?" Easy. Superman.

This is all part of the creation story, and every business, brand, or personality has that creation story that should be made more public.

Cliff Bar is a hundred-million-dollar business that has a story of the founder, Gary Erickson, going on a 175-mile bike ride, and he couldn't stomach another Powerbar.

He decides to go home and concoct a better, all-natural energy bar. And, as they say, the rest is history.

Each year, employees and other friends of the company gather for the "Epiphany Ride" to commemorate that first bike ride when Gary had the idea to create the Cliff Bar.

Maverick1000

For the Maverick1000 network, I relay this story. Maverick1000 began while I was going through a serious entrepreneurial challenge. I had an extremely successful internet business, peer recognition, a wonderful family with two great kids, and more. On the surface, everything was perfect, except I just was not happy. I had stopped growing and stopped being passionate about what I was doing.

These frustrations lead me to do a lot of journaling and reflection.

My discovery was I was happiest when I was actively engaged in three areas (I called them "make more, have more fun, and give more"). And interestingly enough, I found that each of these areas affected the others. For example, the more fun I had, the more my income might go up, or the more I gave, the more income I'd create, etc.

Now, there's no doubt about it—it's lonely at the top. And the only people who truly understand successful entrepreneurs and what we go through are other successful, like-minded entrepreneurs.

That's why I decided to create a small network for other successful entrepreneurs who wanted to live life to the fullest, create business breakthroughs, and have a significant impact through charity and education to empower future entrepreneurs!

I called it Maverick1000, because I believe a small group of 1,000 extraordinary individuals and leaders can (dare I say it?) change the world. Fact is, my faith is in the power of entrepreneurship to create value, innovation, and change. And this invitation-only group of game-changers is designed to support and celebrate your business, personal, and philanthropic achievements and goals, all while having a hell of a lot of fun in the process!

Think about your own creation story.

▸ How did you start your business? What was the inspiration?

▸ What is your reason you do business like you do?

▸ Why do your products/services cost less/more, etc?

Share this with your customers, and you create a deeper connection. In fact, I'd suggest you share the stuff that matters on the outer edges, because there is no money in the middle. You cannot be plain vanilla! My friend Andy Nulman, author of *Pow! Right Between the Eyes* calls these "Velcro®" connections. In his book, he started by revealing ten surprising things about him, and it really bonds the reader. One of the items he mentioned was that he is a hockey goalie. I play ice hockey, and that's one of the ways we bonded when we connected.

INSIDER DISCLOSURE

Going deeper into the Velcro concept Andy talks about, I believe it's about showcasing the good, the bad, and the ugly to really connect with your audience. So on my InternetLifestyle.com blog you might see stories and anecdotes about when I first met my business hero, Sir Richard Branson, things about my kids, business accomplishments, etc.

But you'll also see me dressing up in a chicken suit to go skydiving, watch videos of me running over orange safety cones while F1 racing, and even the story of me falling out of my attic.

You get the whole picture and not just the parts that make me look good. That's one of the things so many companies struggle with, and in this new age of transparency, there cannot be a spin on everything to make you look good.

PRIVILEGES OF INSIDERS

Certainly everyone wants to be an insider, and you can give your customers this advantage in different ways. Johnny Cupcakes is one of the brands that really understands this, because they've built their business on limited edition T-shirts, accessories, and apparel.

Johnny Cupcakes has been approached numerous times by bigger retailers to have their designs in their stores, but so far Johnny Cupcakes has said no. That's one of the biggest thing they've done, is remain authentic to who they are and who their customers are. Many cult brands cater to outliers and their customers appreciate the fact they know about them and not just everybody can wear or own what they do.

Another company that has a similar philosophy is Acid cigars by Drew Estates. The founder, Jonathan Drew, was quoted in *Forbes* as saying, "The day I go mass market, I'm out of business." He gets it. Acid cigars are totally unique because they combine different flavor profiles using ingredients like wine, oil, and herbs. Plus, they are packed in distinctive boxes with limited distribution.

You can reward your customers and make them feel like insiders, too, with special sales, opportunities, and announcements only for them. I like the way Despair.com does this with their annual Blackout sale. They let customers know that anyone visiting the site who is not a customer with insider access will not be able to get into the site at all. There's special sale pricing, but only for insiders.

INSIDER LANGUAGE AND RITUALS

Insiders also have insider language, rituals, secret handshakes, vocab, and slang. If you're talking to internet marketers, acronyms like PPC, EPC, CPA, SEO are pretty commonplace. If you don't know what they mean, you're an outsider.

If you're a Red Wings hockey fan, you know they chuck an octopus onto the ice as a longstanding tradition or ritual during the playoffs.

The secretive and often maligned Freemasons have specific handshakes based on a member's degree; fraternities have their own, as well.

Personally, I find language to be one of the most interesting ways you can create an insider feeling. When people identify themselves as Dead Heads, Trekkies, Parrot Heads, TEDsters, etc., they're making a statement on behalf of the group they belong to and its particular characteristics.

There's no reason you cannot create your own distinguishing name for your fans, too. Gary Vaynerchuk, author of *Crush It*, has anointed his fans "Vayniacs." In fact, UrbanDictionary.com even has a definition: "A crazed, dedicated, wine-loving individual whose day is defined by the visual consumption of their daily fix: a webisode of *The Thunder Show* at winelibrarytv.com, hosted by Gary Vaynerchuk (Vay-Nurr-Chuck!!)."

BEING PART OF THE GROUP

Humans are hard-wired to want to belong. Even if your company is boring as hell, that doesn't mean you cannot create your own army of engaged followers. Check out Fiskateers.com developed for the 200-year-old Fiskars scissor company. Yes, there's not too many people who are scissor zealots, but it's what they do with these scissors that gets customers fired up.

The Brains on Fire agency created a group of "Crafting Ambassadors" for Fiskars. They took hard-core crafting people and provided them with an identity and framework for being true insiders. Each Fiskateer is a given a creed to live up to, they get to review products first, provided they get an ID number. This is an important aspect with Fiskateers being incredibly active online and offline, and they actually identify themselves by their Fiskateer ID number. (A good book to read is *Brains on Fire*, which the founders of the agency wrote.)

PHYSICAL SYMBOL OF INSIDERS

To help spread your message even more, it's ideal to even create some sort of symbol that can be what I call a "conversation crutch." It's something that provides a reason for your converted to talk you up. For example, I have a pair of cuff links shaped like the Virgin Galactic SpaceShipTwo, and I'm always excited to talk about the commercialization of space when someone mentions the cuff links. (I'm actually really bummed because I lost my cuff links at a recent black-tie event. Ugh! So if you got cooler ones, send them my way.)

One of the best examples of a physical symbol is the yellow Livestrong bracelets that appeared on everyone's wrists following their release. This was a simple thing that created massive awareness and an avalanche of imitators. More recently, I really like the symbol from Falling Whistles (Fallingwhistles.com). They have a mission to stop the war in the Congo and the exploitation of children who are too young to fight but are enlisted into the violence with nothing more than a whistle to blow. Supporters wear an actual whistle around their necks, and it's a great conversation piece that opens up the dialogue about the charity.

BEING PART OF SOMETHING BIGGER

Groups are mobilized around a common mission or feeling like they are part of something bigger than them. You can harness this for your business and create brand zealots who spread your message.

One company that really does this well is FEED (www.feedprojects. com). They started with a simple concept: buy one bag and feed one child for a year in a developing country. Boom! Simple idea combined with an outwardly physical symbol (the bag), and you've got a winning combination.

Their idea was simple but profound. Create a fashionable bag that people would want and that also feeds x amount of children per year— hence the name FEED bag. From small beginnings just a few years ago, they've raised millions to feed tens of thousands of children.

Now the big lesson: FEED bag is actually a for-profit enterprise with a social conscience. I love the idea of creating something (that's wanted) with a byproduct for good (e.g., buy a fashionable bag and feed "x" number of children). There is no guilt involved like many charities play on; however, there is strong psychology at work. The bag is very prominently printed with the word FEED on it, and it gives the buyer/ donor a feel-good story to tell others. Plus, anyone else who knows what the bag stands for will recognize the person as having a social conscience. Win-win.

Blake Mycoksie, founder of TOMS® shoes, has a similar model. You buy one pair of shoes, and one pair of shoes goes to a child in need. It's tangible and easy to understand; once again, a wanted product with a charitable byproduct. I see this as one of the most innovative charity models. We saw this a bit with the one-laptop-per-child program, but I don't think that was that big of a hit because not too many people wanted the laptop for themselves or their children. The FEED bag and TOMS shoes are "cool," and that's part of having switched-on fans— they have to believe they are part of something cool!

Some of the most fanatical evangelists are Harley-Davidson owners. You know they're hard-core because you can do a search right now on Google for "Harley tattoos," and you'll find a bunch of people with the logo permanently emblazoned on their skin. In fact, it's a great exercise to think about what it would take to make your brand or company so meaningful that customers would want to tattoo it on their bodies. We had Maverick members in Vegas seriously considering putting the maverick tattoo on themselves for $100. Don't know if it was a joke, but I should have ponied up for it to see what happened.

US VS. THEM

The mentality of either rallying against (or creating) a common enemy is very powerful! In fact, there's a quote for this that goes something like, "Any enemy of my enemy is my friend."

When I was selling to cosmetic surgeons and dermatologists, I always emphasized how managed care was killing their profits and really got them riled up. Or how other unqualified doctors would be competing against them. Here's a paragraph from the sales letter:

Let's face it, nothing beats cosmetic cases.

These patients are the most lucrative and profitable you can ever attract into your practice.

But now, in today's turbulent healthcare field, it seems like everyone and their brother are waking up to this fact. And they're all clamoring for these same rewarding patients. So after taking some weekend course, even a psychiatrist can come back Monday and hang out their shingle as a cosmetic surgeon. What's worse, new scope legislation is trying to move cosmetic surgery into the hands of unqualified doctors competing against you!

People love to side with the Cinderella instead of the wicked stepmother, so let them. A few companies have done this well.

▸ You've got Apple vs. PC
▸ Netflix vs. Blockbuster's late fees and . . .
▸ Voodoo Doughnuts vs. Dunkin Donuts. Huh?

You probably have not heard of Voodoo Doughnuts, but people in Portland love them. They're completely quirky and totally different than the mortal enemy of "normal" doughnuts like Dunkin Donuts. Voodoo doughnuts are fun and whimsical. One of their most popular ones is a doughnut you actually stick with a pretzel "needle" and then bleeds jelly like a voodoo doll. Love it!

There's an interesting article on Neurosciencemarketing.com that cites real scientific proof about Us vs. Them with an experiment by psychologist Henri Tajfel. In the study, Tajfel had groups divide up by somewhat meaningless differences (such as preference of artwork). Then, after being part of a group, those people would provide better rewards to their own group that was formed a few minutes beforehand. Very quickly individuals had become staunch supporters of their group. See http://sozpsy.sowi.uni-mannheim.de/intranet/ php/lecture/files/Tajfel_Billig_Bundy_Flament_1971_EJSP.pdf for the full report.

PERSONALITY

We've talked before about incorporating your company or your own personality into your brand. It's got to be done on a genuine and authentic level. One of my favorite examples are the guys from Killer Shade. This company markets a pretty boring product to other businesses. It sells sun shades. Not exactly sexy like the iPod. But what Killer Shade has done is create a core value of "Being Real."

Here's what they say on their site about it:

> *Be Real: OK kids, here is a fan favorite. We Killers have all had jobs where we had to "fake it," act professional, and put on our "game face" every day we trudged into work. Our little Killer Kingdom was founded on being who we are. When we started January of 2005 we decided that we were going to quit trying to be professional, please everyone and use excellent table manners. In our infinite wisdom, we came to the conclusion that by being who we are we would likely alienate 90 percent of potential customers—but the ones that "got us" would be loyal fans that would allow us to eke out a meager salary while doing what we love. Then the craziest thing happened. People actually liked it. They started coming in droves. Next thing you know—employees loved it, we started attracting the top talent. So what do you end up with— brutally honest people with high integrity that drop the mask. What you see is what you get. We understand we are not a fit for everyone, but we have made our peace, so if you are feelin' our vibe, browse on. If not, best of luck to you . . . try www.boringshade.com.*

And they are pretty authentic in all aspects of their business. In a recruiting video I've seen their operations manager pouring himself a rum and Coke.

I'm always giving you a glimpse into my true personality, and it's definitely not always perfect. I've highlighted things like falling out of my attic or driving 200 mph in a green Speedo. But all of this shows I'm real.

COMMUNITY AND IDENTITY

If you can build a strong sense of community (the buzzword of the early 2000s online), that can propel your brand advocates. Two examples of companies who have done this well are Jones Soda and Threadless.

Jones Soda is the maker of neon-colored, wild-flavored sodas. And their customers have been responsible for everything from the labels on the soda to the sayings under the cap, and even the flavors.

The photographs on the bottles submitted by users (more than 1,000,000!) have been a big driver. People love the photos, and Jones continually changes up the pictures that appear on retail shelves. What's more, in 1999 they started MyJones.com to allow users to create and buy totally personalized bottles from their pictures.

Customers really feel a strong affinity for Jones by the sheer fact they're not mainstream and have their say in it.

Quoted in *BusinessWeek*, founder Peter van Stolk explains, "We allowed the labels to be discovered, and that gave consumers a sense of ownership. It makes it more relevant to them and provides an emotional connection."

COMMUNITY MAKES BUYING DECISIONS

Threadless.com is a perfect "closed loop" system of interactivity, feedback, and direct sales back to your group. It's pretty damn smart! They have more than 300,000 registered users who vote on T-shirt designs submitted by other users in the community. The shirts that get the best scores are the ones that are produced and sold right back to the group who said they wanted to buy it. Those that don't make the cut are banished to the design archives.

The winners get fame (sort of) and fortune (sort of). They'll receive a cash prize if they get their T-shirt selected for printing and their design immortalized. Actually, it's pretty cool because on the T-shirt I bought, the designer's name is on the back tag, too.

Let's Explore This a Little More

First off, there is almost no risk in using this type of system. It's a perfect closed loop with material submitted by users, voted on by users, and then purchased by the users. This is one of the best applications of the online world I've seen in quite some time. Consider how much less risk there is in letting your community tell you exactly what they want to purchase and then giving it right back to them. Actually, I would bet the sales are even better because the users feel like they are involved from the very first step. They feel like they have their hand in the birthing of the T-shirt.

Now the guys behind Threadless.com have only the risk of printing up too much inventory, but I'm sure they've got that figured based on the scoring the T-shirts received and past sales numbers.

Also, they have an ingenious built-in feature that lets would-be buyers request a reprint of a shirt if it's sold out already. You provide your email address and which size T-shirt you want to get updates if your favorite design will be updated and or reprinted. Their website's shop also leaves up lots of their sold-out designs, which shows "social proof" of other people buying. Plus, it gets people submitting their info to be notified of reprints (once again diminishing the risk of excess inventory).

Threadless.com works on so many levels involving their users and really building community, which keeps them involved and excited about the T-shirts. Plus, it continues building social proof of how cool their designs are.

They let users post photos of themselves wearing the T-shirt designs. The more you see people in the T-shirt, the "cooler" you think it is. Plus, it allows members of the community to get a bit of recognition and fame. They also get "points" for submitting their photo in a T-shirt design.

Keeping it fun and quirky, if you start glancing through the T-shirts (yes, I just bought another one!), you'll see the staff at Threadless.com really gets into the photography of the shirt. There's a design with

Darth Vader of *Star Wars* pruning a tree. It's pretty good, but then take a look at the product pic. There's a guy shearing another team member's hair (while wearing the T-shirt).

Maverick Library

Here are some books to read for further info:

▶ *Primal Branding* by Patrick Hanlon. Hanlon comes from the big agency world but nevertheless I really think his seven components are important to run through the bootstrappers' lenses: "The creation of story"; "the creed"; "the icons"; "the rituals"; "pagans (nonbelievers)"; "sacred words"; "the leader". All of this works together.

▶ *Brains on Fire* by Phillips, Cordell, Church and Jones. I'm not sure where I stumbled onto the *Brains on Fire* blog, but I'm glad I found it. *Brains on Fire* has some really awesome stuff when it comes to creating movements for your customers, advocates, and zealots. They've done a superb job of breaking down the ten elements that go into the mix for creating movements and tight communities.

With traditional media having less impact, it may be time for marketers to stop defaulting to the yo-yo of advertising campaigns and instead really look to "ignite" a word-of-mouth movement. Some of the advice here really hits home for the conversations that are taking place around your business or brand driven from the bottom up.

The *Brains on Fire* crew hands you ten rules for how they've engineered self-sustaining and extremely passionate (and successful) movements like the Fiskateers and Rage Against the Haze for anti-smoking in South Carolina. Those are the two you hear the most about in the book and both are worthy of case studies by themselves.

Maverick Library, continued

▶ *True Believer* by Eric Hoffer. The is the premier guide book on building and starting your own cult. While we don't necessarily want our customers lacing up Nikes and waiting for the comet to take them away, some of these elements are very powerful when applied.

X-Factor 8

WHAT'S NEXT?

TAKE YOUR CUSTOMER BY THE HAND—AND SHOW THEM THE WAY!

Here's something that you should immediately put into action.

This concept is so simple, yet most of the time extremely overlooked. Here it is: With every single transaction (i.e., opt-in, registration, or purchase), you should be controlling where your customer goes next. I see so many people missing out on this golden opportunity for additional profit. For instance, the thank-you page after an order might only say, "Thank you for your order—it will be shipped out soon."

Dumb!!

Where's that customer going to go now? We have no frickin' idea, but I would doubt it's back to one of your other sites to spend more money with you. But they could (and will) if you give them the opportunity.

What about after someone opts-in to one of your mail lists, maybe, like a priority notification list? The page probably says *Thank you—please look for _____ in your email box shortly.*

Dumb da dum dumb!

Another opportunity lost. Hopefully, you've got my drift by now. There are so many little tiny "profit leverage" points on your website, and this is one of the easiest to increase any transaction.

Let me show you a few examples so you really get it and see how many places you can use this technique.

THANK-YOU PAGE AFTER AN ORDER

If someone just whipped out their credit card, they are way more likely to spend again if you give them an opportunity and an incentive. I know it seems to go against common sense, but the old-school, direct-marketing formula is RFM: recency, frequency, and monetary value. This is one reason why direct-marketing companies are looking for "hot line" names when they rent other mail order buyers lists. Those are the most recent purchasers of a particular product.

On your thank-you page, you've got people at one of their most responsive points.

Here's an example of a thank-you page after someone grabs our Public Domain Goldmine product. They've already spent up to several hundred dollars, and now they've got a $200 discount for another, related product. It only takes a few paragraphs for 10.5 percent of the customers to buy an additional $497 course. See Figure 8.1.

Trust me, this works all the time for a related product at a discounted price. The thank-you page offer from VistaPrint gives you an opportunity to get additional magnets just like your business card at a discount if you order within ten minutes.

And what if you don't have another product to sell? No problem either.

Your thank-you page could easily be used for affiliate offers. My buddy John Reese used to have a five-page thank you that explained his

> **Thank you for your order, ((First Name))!**
>
> It will be shipped out to you immediately (international customers please allow extra shipping time).
>
> If you need any help or have any questions please go here: www.surefiremarketing.com/support/
>
> ---
>
> ### If You Want Extra Help – Here's The Most Comprehensive Step-by-Step Guide to Profiting From The Public Domain
>
> #### (And You'll Save $200.00)
>
> Others paid $1,995.00 for this but it's yours for a fraction of the price right now:
> Since releasing the Public Domain Riches program I've been getting flooded with emails and phone calls asking (sometimes even begging) me to create some kind of advanced "hold-you-by-the-hand" program for profiting from the public domain.
>
> Originally I introduced this material s a private "online workshop" for $1,995.00 per person and the response was so overwhelming that all four classes we offered completely SOLD OUT within a few days! Now I've taken this material and turned into a comprehensive home study course since I don't know when the next live workshops will be held.
>
> Public Domain Riches Quantum Leap home study program is an entire 8-week system that takes you every step of the way, from uncovering and evaluating possible public domain material, analyzing markets with you, creating sales copy, helping set up joint ventures, getting the whole thing on auto pilot giving you the "kick-in-the-butt" you need to get going. The complete **Quantum Leap home study package is yours today for only $497** in addition to the price of Public Domain Riches Gold Mine - regularly selling on our site for $697 but you save $200.00 because you are buying everything now).
>
> After each lesson you are giving simple homework assignments to make sure you stay on track. Now once you've mastered these steps - it's the closest thing I know to legally creating your own automatic money machine by "stealing" a product from the public domain. And you can do this over and over and over again once you see how to do it the right way with Yanik Silver as your guide.
>
> **Plus you get the biggest extra bonus of all, you'll get to watch me in real-time do the exact same thing you're doing.** You'll get 39 full-length screen capture videos on CD-rom. I'll be working "without a net" and going through the identical process you're doing. My public domain project has absolutely nothing to do with advertising, marketing, Internet marketing, or making money. I don't even have a list of people interested in this so I come in with a blank slate and probably start exactly where you are beginning.
>
> This will be like a real-time laboratory experiment you can watch and learn from. (I plan on selling these **"watch-me-then-you-do-it"** screen capture videos separately for $295.00 but it is another free gift for you right now).
>
> Here's a quick comment on these videos from a student:
>
> "...I think you are the perfect teacher. You know what people like....step by step instructions followed by videos to guide and further instruct you. The videos are tremendously valuable. I watch those over and over because you always pick up something that you may have missed the first time. And of course, you forget. I think the course is well laid out. Right now, I can't think of anything that it's lacking..." - **Linda Kajda, Harwich, MA**
>
> **Click Here to Get Your $200
> Quantum Leap Discount Now!**

FIGURE 8.1 Use your thank-you page to sell another product

story and then recommended additional products for sale, which he got an affiliate commission for.

OK, those are easy enough, but here are two more.

THANK-YOU PAGE AFTER OPT-IN

Another overlooked spot for so many sites is the opt-in page confirmation or thank-you page. With almost every email auto-responder company you can specify what the "success" or "confirmation'" page will be. Unless you're doing a forced opt-in capture and then sending people to the sales page, you can put some sort of offer on the thank-you page. This works incredibly well for any type of priority notification list or some sort of "early bird list," where the page is only designed to get people to leave their info to get ready for a launch. Don't miss this opportunity to send them somewhere else.

Go back through each of your sites and think about where there are overlooked profit opportunities on the thank-you, opt-in, and registration pages. I promise this one idea will be worth at least 100 times what you paid for this book.

CAPTURING AND USING BIRTHDAYS

This is going to be one of those moments when you slap yourself on the head and say, "Why didn't I think of this?!"

Everybody loves to be remembered on their birthday. I'd bet you're no different. Usually the only people that give you birthday cards are your parents, your spouse, or your sister. (Though with Facebook you'll get a bunch of wall posts—but they don't really count.)

In Harvey Mackay's book, *Swim with the Sharks Without Being Eaten Alive*, he asks if there is any coincidence the Mackay Envelope Company (Harvey's company) gets some of their biggest orders from customers when sales reps call on the day of their birthday.

Recently I've been experimenting with capturing birthdays on the bottom of our order forms. It just says, "Optional: Let us know your birthday (just month and day) and you'll get a special surprise from us on your big day.

We only ask for the month and day since we don't want people feeling weird about giving out their year. We're getting about 47 percent of customers to give up this info at the point of sale.

The special birthday gift they get is a downloadable package of goodies on a private page . . . plus a discount on some of our products. Here's the page, in Figures 8.2 and 8.3.

Now, I don't want these pages up forever, so I had my tech person set it up so the link only works for one month. That's it.

Right before the beginning of the month I send out a spreadsheet of all the upcoming month's birthdays to my mail house. They then personalize birthday cards for our customers that go out in a real

FIGURE 8.2 Don't miss the opportunity in customer birthdays

envelope. We send the cards out twice a month so the birthdays after the 15th of the month get sent in the second batch. Here's what they look like, in Figure 8.4, page 104.

For Maverick members, we use SendOutCards.com for the birthday greeting cards, and we include a pack of brownies or another small gift.

My friend Rory Fatt teaches restaurant owners how to use birthdays in their marketing and it always is the biggest promotion they do. The secret is to acknowledge and give a special offer just for them. I'd love to hear your results and any twists on it.

EXTRA BONUS
Birthday GIFT!

Not only do you get that special collection of goodies – but you can also save 20% on our best-selling resources and tools....good during your Birthday Month!

To order simply check the box for each product(s) you'd like and then hit submit to be taken to our safe and secure online order form.

Note: For more information you can click on the link for the product. But don't order off the main page or you'll have to pay regular price. All items come with their full guarantee period and also ALL the bonuses.

Copywriting Information:

☐ Yanik Silver's Ultimate 'At-Home' Internet Copywriting Workshop
Here's the masters course on copywriting. Over 1579 pages of fully-indexed material from the $3,975.00 per person LIVE copywriting workshop. You get it all for a fraction of the cost.

Your mastery of copywriting is the ultimate form of financial security and profit potential. It doesn't matter what kind of business you have or what you sell - copywriting is the skill that WILL be of the greatest value to you.

Just $1180 (Normally - $1475) – you save 20%
Read about it here: http://www.ultimatecopywritingworkshop.com/preview_thanks.shtml

FIGURE 8.3 Special birthday discounts for customers

FIGURE 8.4 Sample birthday card

A Simple Fold-Up Birthday Card Makes a Big Impression

"Happy Birthday to you . . .

"Happy Birthday to you . . .

"Happy Birthday . . . dear [Firstname] . . .

Happy Birthday to you!!!"

[Firstname], trust me, you wouldn't want me to sing it to you
(just pretend I did) 😎

I wanted to wish you a wonderful birthday and give you a special gift
of "birthday goodies." You can pick them up here (but hurry
because they're only there during your birthday month).

http://www.blahblah

Have a great Bday!

—Yanik Silver & Your Friends at SurefireMarketing.com

CASHING IN ON EVENTS AND BREAKING NEWS

As Mavericks we have the opportunity to ensure our customers are always excited about "What's next?" and create that feeling of fun anticipation. An easy way to stop being boring is to use out-of-the-norm events for your marketing. A lot of people might do sales or events based on typical calendar dates like Christmas or New Year's, but I doubt many of us do Flag Day sales, right?

Take a look at this example I saw just recently from Betabrand. They're a somewhat quirky brand that started with "cordaround" pants.

Those are corduroy pants that are horizontal instead of vertical. So for Flag Day they piggybacked perfectly on the theme by offering 17.76 percent off their red, white, and blue products. (Get it?)

Pretty smart and clever.

In our 24/7 society, you should be fleet of foot and click to capitalize. I saw OoVoo.com, which does group online video chat and competes against Skype. They put out a promo saying they'd give away a day of their service for every hour Skype was down.

The offer is extremely time sensitive with Skype being down (which I didn't even know until they sent it). Pretty smart.

For the Super Bowl a few years ago, I wanted to capitalize on the conversation in our customers' heads with a fun promotion. (Side note: The NFL actually heavily scrutinizes and goes after people using the word "Super Bowl" and the actual names of the teams, etc. So that's why I called it the "Big Game.") See Figure 8.5.

It worked (sorta).

Here's the breakdown.

Once people got to the page, there was a place for them to pick either Indianapolis or Chicago as the winning team, and predict the half-time and final score. Because I was under a deadline to promote the Underground III's final price break, I only got the Super Bowl email out on game day. I think that was a mistake. My original intention was to do it a week ahead and hit the list a few times with it. Take a look at that email below.

Super Bowl Email

{!firstname_fix}, who's going to win the "Big Game" today?

Hey {!firstname_fix},

Yanik Silver here with something kinda fun on this "Super Sunday."

If you're even slightly a football fan, then your TV is tuned in to the "Big Game" today! Of course, I'm talking about Chicago vs. Indianapolis.

FIGURE 8.5 Engaging customers with the existing conversation

Now usually I just watch every year for the amusing commercials but figured this year I'd do something fun to keep everyone more interested (in between munching on some pizza and downing a few brews!) ;)

I'm giving away a bunch of autographed football memorabilia—everything from helmets to balls to jerseys, and more!

Just head over here to see what this is all about at

www.surefiremarketing.com/prediction/

It's easy to win, just give me your best prediction for the winning team's score at half-time and then end of the game. Don't worry, even if you're wrong, you'll still have a chance for prizes and discounts in our random draw.

Check it out!

www.surefiremarketing.com/prediction/

—Yanik "Grid Iron" Silver

P.S. Do it now, because obviously this fun little contest turns off once the game starts ;)

I got roughly 450 people to predict the score in this contest, and then on the thank-you page was an offer for a trial to our Secret Society newsletter. We got nine people to sign up, which translates to about $4K in revenue over the course of the year if 50 percent of those subscriptions stay. Here's the thank-you page with the football theme continued. See Figure 8.6.

I decided to send real-time updates to the winners during the Super Bowl. So when the Colts were up after halftime, here's what those prediction winners were sent:

Prediction Winners Email

{!firstname_fix}—Half-time winner!

Hey {!firstname_fix},

Congratulations, you won!

You're one of our Big Game Half-time prediction winners.

Nice work! (Hey—I could use you for some of my stock picks) ;)

Special Trial Offer

<u>FREE</u>Underground Secret Society

Charter Membership for 1 Month

FIGURE 8.6 Giving them the "What's Next" opportunity on the opt-in "success" page

Go Colts!

Be on the look out for a separate email if you are one of our grand prize winners for autographed football memorabilia. You've got a great chance of winning since the grand prize drawings are only from the group of winners. (Right now it stands at six people!)

What's more, you've already won our biggest discount on our Super Sale!

Here's the page:

www.surefiremarketing.com/prediction/biggame.html

Use coupon code "biggame250" to get another $250.00 off the already reduced prices on some of our best-selling resources.

OK, now, back to the game and more wings! Yum!

—Yanik

Notice the coupon code for the sale page. I had a $75-, a $150-, and a $250-off coupon. I'll show you where I used this in a second. For now, here's the sales page we directed people to with a 48-hour countdown timer. See Figure 8.7.

I had this email ready to go ahead of time and could just substitute Bears or Colts. (Personally, I wanted the Bears to win since my in-laws are from Chicago. And it looked good after that first kickoff return for a touchdown—but not to be.)

FIGURE 8.7 Time-sensitive special deal letter

Then, after the game, here are the other emails that went out to the final score winner (just one guy, but I'll show you something later that totally surprised me), the people who predicted the Colts, and then the Bears fans.

Email to Winner of Final Score

{!firstname_fix}, you predicted the right score!

Congratulations {!firstname_fix}!

You won!

You're one of our Big Game prediction winners.

Nice work! (Hey—I could use you for some of my stock picks) ;)

Go Colts!

Be on the look out for a separate email if you are one of our grand prize winners for autographed football memorabilia. You've got a great chance of winning since the grand prize drawings are only from the group of winners.

What's more, you've already won our biggest discount on our Super Sale!

Here's the page:

www.surefiremarketing.com/prediction/biggame.html

Use coupon code "biggame250" to get $250.00 off the already reduced prices on some of our bestselling resources.

Now please pass me the TUMS after all those beers and pizza! ;)

—Yanik

Here's the email to people who predicted the Colts to win:

{!firstname_fix}, you predicted the winning team!

Hi {!firstname_fix},

Congratulations you won!

You're one of our Big Game prediction winners for picking the Colts to win it.

Those odds makers in Vegas have nothing on you! ;)

Be on the look out for a separate email if you are one of our grand prize winners for autographed football memorabilia. You've got a great chance of winning since the grand prize drawings are only from the group of winners.

For now, you've won a discount on our Super Sale!

Here's the page:

www.surefiremarketing.com/prediction/biggame.html

Use coupon code "win150" to get $150.00 off the already reduced prices on some of our bestselling resources.

Now please pass me the TUMS after all those beers and pizza! ;)

Best,

Yanik Silver

SurefireMarketing.com

And, finally the email to the Bears predictions:

{!firstname_fix}, sorry–Chicago didn't win (but you still did)!

Hi {!firstname_fix}

Tough break!

The game tonight was really wild and it looked good after the initial kickoff. :)

Even though Chicago didn't win, you're still a 2nd-place winner! That's right, the good news is you've won a nice discount on the Super Sale we're running for 48 hours.

Here's the page:

www.surefiremarketing.com/prediction/biggame.html

Use coupon code "super75" to get $75.00 off the already reduced prices on some of our best-selling resources.

Now please pass me the TUMS after all those beers and pizza! ;)

All the best,

Yanik Silver,

SurefireMarketing.com

P.S. There may be more good news . . . you are still in the running for a random draw for some of the autographed football memorabilia. We'll let you know via a separate email if you win that!

I think the last two letters are really important. Most people, if they do a contest, only notify the winners. Dumb! Like for instance, you've all seen those fish bowls in restaurants telling you that you can win a free lunch for your office (or whatever) if you just drop in your business card. Well, I'd say 95 percent of restaurants just toss out the non-winning cards. Hmmm . . .

So, if you notice, no matter who they were—they won! I showed you previously we had three different coupons codes, and it's only fair for the people who did the best in the contest to get a better discount.

Now, here comes another cool part of the promo. I drove people back to the sales page to find out if they won one of the prizes. The bigger prizes were drawn for people who predicted the right score, but the smaller prizes like the hats were randomly drawn from everyone who entered. That way, even if they lost, they could still win a prize.

Here's the email that sent them back to the sales page/winner's page:

{!firstname_fix} – Big Game prediction winners posted

Hi {!firstname_fix},

Thanks and congratulations on making the right prediction for the winning team from the Big Game this weekend.

Check to see if you've won any of our cool, football collectibles.

www.surefiremarketing.com/prediction/winners.html

What's more, you've already won a big discount on our Super Sale!

It's all on the same page:

www.surefiremarketing.com/prediction/winners.html

Use coupon code "win150" to get $150 off the already reduced prices on some of our best-selling resources.

You have to get there fast, because the sale ends in less than nine hours!

Best,

Yanik Silver

And the people who predicted the Bears got the same thing, but slightly revised and with a different coupon code again for $75 off.

Now, here's the winners page (and after all the prizes are listed with the winners, the sales page was right below it again) in Figures 8.8 and 8.9 on pages 115 and 116.

An interesting side note: About ten minutes before the game ended, I went to eBay.com and started buying up a bunch of Colts collectible and autographed merchandise. I figured the prices on some stuff like the Peyton Manning signed jersey that I got would go up immediately after the Super Bowl was over.

The Envelope, Please

Now for some results and the Monday morning quarterbacking. We got a couple thousand in sales from products sold on the sales page, and together with the new Secret Society members it was OK, profit-wise. Definitely not one of my best, but I think it could have been a ten times bigger promo if I did a few things differently:

- ▸ Mailed more and mailed sooner
- ▸ Sent the email more in advance of the big day. (Sunday morning isn't ideal.)

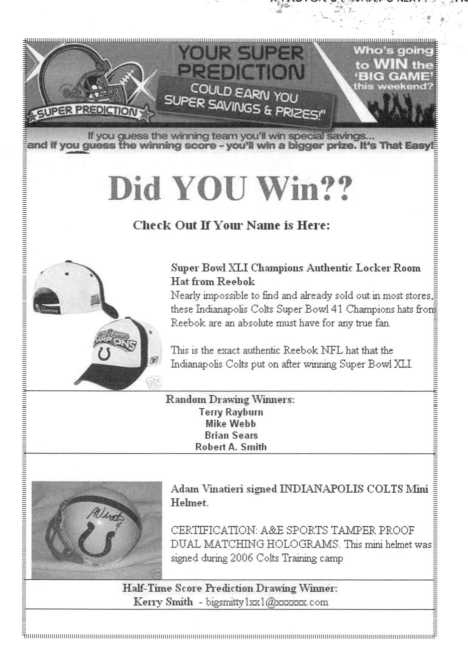

FIGURE 8.8 The winners page

GRAND PRIZE!
Peyton Manning,
Super Bowl XLI MVP,
signed jersey

In 1998, Peyton Manning completed one of the finest rookie seasons ever played by a quarterback, passing for 3,739 yards and 26 touchdowns! He has since become one of the best quarterbacks in the NFL today. Through his first six seasons with the Colts, Peyton averaged more than 4,000 passing yards and 27 touchdown passes per season! With a cannon for an arm he can cut through the best defenses in the NFL, he has a chance to become one of the best quarterbacks to ever play in the NFL!

This is a full size Indianapolis Colts Jersey, signed by, Peyton Manning!

This is an "Authentic" jersey, made with sewn-on name & numbers just like Peyton wears on the field! Peyton has hand-signed this jersey boldly to make a truly incredible collectible! Retail Value is $600!

Grand Prize Winner -- Winning Final Game Score:
Jeremy Cockerill -- jeremyx@universabxxxxxxe.com

Important: If you're one of the winners please submit a ticket at www.surefiremarketing.com/support with your shipping address and the item you won so we can send it off to you!

Don't worry if you didn't win -- you can still get SUPER savings on some of our best-selling resources below...

Sales Page Again

YANIK "GRIDIRON" SILVER

"Beat the Clock & Claim Your 'Super' Discount On Some of Our Best-Selling Products!"

FIGURE 8.9 Reminding nonwinners they still have something to gain

> ▸ Gave people a reason to pass along the page to their friends. (i.e., another entry into the contest for every friend that enters or comes to the page, etc.). That's pretty easy to do but I didn't have enough time to set that up. I recommend Tell-a-Friend Pro (www.TAFPro.com) if you want to do this.
>
> ▸ Added some sort of affiliate component to it, so that affiliates would get credit for sales on the thank-you page and the Super Sale.

▸ Use the press. My initial idea was to try and get some good PR from it by telling the media I knew the winner of the game and even the winning score based on some calculations that people gave me. I think this could have really got some good press and I'm kicking myself for not doing it earlier. The media loves predictions and it would be perfect to piggyback on a major news story like the Super Bowl. (Oh well, there's always next year!)

Interestingly enough, now that I had a chance to look at the data from people who entered the contest, it's incredibly accurate. First, 72 percent of people picked the Colts to win. Not a huge surprise there, since they were favored, but here's the cool part: If I took an average of the scores people gave me for their predictions, they were within one or two points of the actual score! I think that's pretty amazing!

The halftime score for the Colts was 16 and the average predicted was 14.2 (so 14). And then the winning prediction average was 27.9 (so 28) and the real winning score was 29! I bet with even more people in the contest it would get better. I have no idea if 307 predictions is statistically valid (probably not), but it's the whole "Wisdom of Crowds" theory applied.

Now, the reason I gave you so much detail in here is not so you can do a Super Bowl promo next year (you can), but it's to get you thinking about events and things that are in people's minds. Remember, enter the conversation already taking place and see how you can turn that into a promotion opportunity.

INSTEAD OF: "WHAT'S NEXT?"
TRY: "WHAT HAPPENED BEFORE?"

Here's something else to file away. You don't always have to have a chronological "what's next" available. Look at the blockbuster *Star Wars* trilogy. After 16 years, George Lucas went back and created a prequel to *Star Wars* with another three episodes showing the back story of the Jedi knights. All-in the franchise has grossed more than $4 billion in box office sales.

X-Factor 9

CONNECTING AND TAPPING YOUR MASTERMIND

HOW TO CREATE A POWERFUL NETWORK

Everybody has heard the expression, "It's not what you know, but who you know that counts."

That's partially true, and I'd have to say the ability to create high-level connections has been a big factor in my success over the past ten years, but I've never really shared exactly how I think about this.

First off, I really don't like the word "networking" to describe making a connection. That conjures up the image of somebody walking into a mixer and slinging their business cards around like some two-for-one Red Lobster coupon. Or going to events that have "speed networking" aspects where you glad-hand three dozen people and ask them "What do you do? How can I help you?"

All of this strikes me as being somewhat cheesy!

So What Do You Do?

▶ *Be genuine.* I've watched some of my friends, like Joe Polish, who I think are incredible at their connections and it comes from a real genuineness. I see Joe tell really silly jokes and just be himself. That's really refreshing. Personally, I've been known to buy a couple dozen shots and start handing them out at the bar during an event. It totally fits my personality, plus it gets people who I wouldn't normally meet to say "Hello" to me.

  When I talk to people I've just met, I look for any connections we have outside of work. In fact, I purposefully do not ask, "What do you do?" unless they ask me first. Of course, I'm interested, but I'd rather find out something unusual about them.

▶ *Make introductions.* The other thing I consciously think about is who in my existing network I can introduce to foster a connection. This is a trait some of the best connectors I know do: They are extremely generous with introductions where it makes sense.

▶ *Be distinctive.* My friend and business coach, Cameron Herold, former COO of 1-800-Got-Junk, told me about how his team would wear blue logoed vests at seminars and events. People would stop them and ask what 1-800-Got-Junk did, or what it was, and it was a really good way to stand out. The metal business cards for Maverick Business Adventures stand out and get people showing them around to others at a meeting.

▶ *Get diverse.* Some of my favorite connections have come out of charities I support, hobbies, or different interests. There's a different connection formed with a common interest first and business second. What's more, if you have a shared intense experience you'll have a much deeper connection. I think that's one of the reasons Maverick members have done so many deals together and are so eager to help each other. It's a deeper bond than simply meeting a person at a seminar or event.

- *Become prolific and prominent.* This probably isn't that big of a secret but worth mentioning. If you can get on stage, write a book, become an expert, etc., you'll have people seeking you out.
- *Follow-up.* I admit I don't do this as well as I could, but I shoot quick texts or emails or clippings over to people when I know it's something they're interested in.

Another high-level practice I've used to make connections and push my business forward is by harnessing the power of MasterMind groups.

MASTERMIND GROUPS

"If you can grasp this principle and apply it you may have,
for your efforts, whatever you want on this earth!"

Those are the words of Napoleon Hill, who first coined the term "MasterMind" in his widely regarded *Think & Grow Rich* and *Law of Success* works.

In case you don't know the story, Hill was commissioned by Andrew Carnegie to interview 500 successful men and women, looking for the secret to success. One of the key concepts he discovered was the power of a MasterMind group. Every titan of industry from Henry Ford to Thomas Edison to William Wrigley, Jr. all tapped into this either "by accident or design," as Hill says.

I've been part of multiple MasterMind groups and run several for the past four years. I'll share the different ways they've worked and also how to set up your own.

WHY YOU NEED A MASTERMIND GROUP

Personally, I can count at least $2 million in revenue that came from ideas generated from my own private MasterMind groups that I never would have figured out on my own. What's more, my first dream car (Mercedes SL55) was bought and paid for just from one single idea conceived at a MasterMind meeting. Another idea has turned into a $45,000 monthly revenue stream.

And yet another idea (really a tiny tweak) was directly responsible for $290,000 in sales during two weekends. Those are just a few of the ideas that come to mind immediately. I'm sure if pressed I could recount even more big ideas that came as a direct impact of being part of a MasterMind group.

On top of the breakthrough ideas, there are many more reasons a MasterMind can help you reach new levels in your business.

- ▶ *Speed*. Imagine the speed that comes from tapping into the collective brain trust of experience and results here. For instance, if you had 12 people in the group testing one new thing in their business each month, that's 12 x 12 = 144 new breakthroughs. It would take you 144 months on your own to be able to get the same information.

- ▶ *Competitiveness*. There's a certain friendly "competitive spirit" among the MasterMind group because nobody wants to show up to a meeting without something to "brag on" or with successes to share. It's this competitiveness that drives results even further that the group benefits from.

- ▶ *Increased productivity*. A MasterMind group empowers you to become more than you are now. At the meetings you are surrounded by other successful entrepreneurs who spark new ideas and fresh energy!

- ▶ *Accountability*. Each MasterMind member gets even more accomplished because of feeling accountable to the group for their actions and progress.

- ▶ *Group feeling*. When a MasterMind group has been properly selected, each person is cooperating and cheerleading for your best results, efforts, and "best self" to step forward. Quite frankly, it's pretty lonely being a top-performing entrepreneur, so having a group of successful peers who understand you is incredibly important.

▶ *New resources and contacts*. It's not unusual to walk from meetings with a notebook full of new contacts and resources. A Master-Mind group lets you tap into shared contacts and unique expertise from other like-minded members.

▶ *New perspectives*. Each member brings with them a new perspective, model, or frame of reference to an issue or idea. It's exactly these kinds of fresh insights that lead to big breakthroughs instead of looking at a situation through the same filter.

I've been part of informal and formal MasterMind groups, and typically it works much better when there is some formality to it, because that usually increases commitment. If you're interested in starting your own group, you must make sure there is serious commitment and consequences for missing meetings. I've been part of groups that meet once a month or quarter, and I've found that for extremely busy and successful individuals, the three or four times per year in person is ideal.

When I was getting started, some of my friends and I started a local group that met once a month, and that was too much. We then moved to about every other month and that worked better. Then, as we got more successful, we moved to a quarterly structure and then we slowly dissolved the group.

It's not to say the monthly meeting can't work, but normally, at the highest level, people's schedules are so hectic that it becomes extremely tough to make happen.

I've also been part of two different internet MasterMind groups that don't have a set meeting schedule and simply run via an email list. For asking quick questions, getting resources, or trading junior high jokes, this is a simple format that has benefits.

Having been part of so many different groups and seen which ones worked and which ones didn't, I'll give you a few pointers:

▶ Confidentiality within the group is imperative. (High trust factor among the group to share important information.)

- True peer-to-peer connections with a qualification process (i.e., startups and seven-figure-revenue business owners don't typically have the same issues.) A MasterMind group is not a mentor relationship but a true peer-to-peer releation.
- Be open and focus on giving, not just taking, value.
- Commit to the group.

The two MasterMind groups I run have a simple (but powerful) format. Each member gets approximately 50 minutes to present something that is working well in their business that other members can use for their own businesses. Then, during the second half of their presentation time they present a problem or opportunity for the group to help with.

Maverick Resource

MasterMind members consist of business owners with a seven-figure business or within striking distance of seven figures. More details are here: www.surefiremarketing.com/mastermind.

MENTORS AND THOUGHT PROVOKERS

I always believe it's the people you meet, books you read, and experience you have that influence your life. I learned from Earl Nightingale early on about books, resources, and educational material as a "mentorship," but I've always been lucky enough to surround myself with, meet, and interview influential thinkers. I look for their philosophies about life, business, and achievement, and keep everything in a journal that I continually re-read.

X-Factor 10

CREATE THE FUN

MAVERICK RULE 31 SAYS "MAKE YOUR BUSINESS AND DOING BUSINESS WITH YOU FUN!"

I'm a big believer in having a lot of fun in how you work and how you play (Maverick Rules are part of my book, *34 Rules for Maverick Entrepreneurs*, www.internetlifestyle.com/blog/ramblings/33-rules-for-maverick-entrepreneurs).

As a self-described "adventure junkie," I've found my own life-changing experiences—running with the bulls, bungee jumping, sky diving, exotic car rallies, Baja racing, zero-gravity flights, etc.—have not only brought a profound sense of accomplishment but also led to breakthroughs in ideas, focus, and business thinking. Trust me, you don't have to get as extreme as I do sometimes, but you do need to break out of your typical routine. Fresh thinking and big ideas come from new experiences away from the office! Plus, as you open yourself up to new adventures or experiences, it opens up different ways of thinking about issues in your business (and life).

LET'S START

By and large, most people's businesses are B-O-R-I-N-G! I'm talking Zzzzzzzzz City! Even the good sales letter sites do not use this technique to breathe life into their site beyond the typical benefit-driven headline, subheads, etc.

I'm talking giving your site (and yourself) a unique personality in the marketplace. First, let's talk about giving a site a personality. Here are two of my favorite examples: www.Demotivation.com and www.Despair.com.

The personality of being sarcastic, entertaining, and against the grain comes out just about everywhere on both their sites.

From the FAQs about their book *The Art of Demotivation*:

Q: Is this book for real?

A: As sure as the ISBN is 1-892503-40-9, this book is for real. If you don't believe us, order a copy and watch as our real financial department really charges your real credit card for 30 real dollars.

Q: Is it possible to get Dr. Kersten's autograph on my copy of the book?

A: Dr. Kersten autographs each and every Chairman Edition of *The Art of Demotivation* with a personal message. He can't be bothered with Manager or Executive Editions. Money talks, yo.

The Art of Demotivation book comes in three editions, up to the $1,195 Executive Edition.

Now, on Despair.com they also sell some of my favorite prints, which are the opposite of "Successories." I bought some for my friends this year for the holidays. They are hilarious! One I bought my buddy Bill says "Achievement" with a picture of the pyramids. And then underneath, the caption is "You Can Do Anything You Set Your Mind to When You Have Vision, Determination, and an Endless Supply of Expendable Labor."

Now, a true personality for your website has to be carried through in all the little communications with customers and prospects. To see how far they take their personality, fill out a "troubled ticket" and you'll get back the response "Now Firing. The pink slips are being drafted as we speak."

They really have this personality plugged into every nook and cranny of their website. I love it!

Now, you might be thinking that you'll repel some customers and people will get a little pissed off after this type of treatment. The answer is absolutely yes! And that's a good thing, because you don't want to be plain vanilla if you are in heavily competitive marketplaces. Go ahead and polarize your prospects and customers to either love you or hate you. There's no money to be made in the middle. Look at Howard Stern. There are people who absolutely love him and now pay SiriusXM radio a monthly subscription just to listen to their "god." But on the other hand, there are a lot of people, too, who will tune in just to see what Howard says so they can hate him more.

A FEW MORE SITES WITH PERSONALITY

CDBaby.com doesn't quite go as far, but it tells you in no uncertain terms you're not dealing with a conglomerate. Check out the personality that comes through in their emails about when your CD ships:

> Thanks for your order with CD Baby! Your CD has been gently taken from our CD Baby shelves with sterilized contamination-free gloves and placed onto a satin pillow.
>
> A team of 50 employees inspected your CD and polished it to make sure it was in the best possible condition before mailing. Our packing specialist from Japan lit a candle and a hush fell over the crowd as he put your CD into the finest gold-lined box that money can buy.

THEMED MARKETING FOR MAVERICKS

One of the biggest issues most businesses have is how to stop being BORING!

You want your customers and prospects to be thinking, "Wow! What's this crazy guy (or gal) going to do next?"

It's no secret that the majority of your customers and prospects live somewhat typical lives. So it's not enough anymore just to present an offer filled with benefits, it's also got to entertain them and be exciting.

I'm going to let you step behind some of my bestselling campaigns that all involved themes. Now, don't think you need to create some sort of corny, fake image that's not really you—you don't. You want to keep it fun and keep the sales message in the forefront of your prospect's mind.

Let's start with my very first one: that was "Yanik's 30th Birthday Bash!"

I decided I was going to hold a super blowout party for my 30th birthday and invite all my best customers and prospects to it. More than 531 people came to my little birthday party (see Figure 10.1), and it was the biggest internet-marketing-only seminar at that time.

I brainstormed what a birthday has and then planned my promotion and actual event around it. People everywhere love to have fun! Entertainment is something people spend their last nickel on because everyone wants to have fun.

THE BIRTHDAY BASH

First, starting with the promotion. Here's the first page of the sales letter—notice me in the goofy birthday hat. See Figure 10.1.

A few guys on my hockey team saw this picture and gave me a hell of a time at the next game we had. But the picture really fits perfectly. You may or may not want to be this "goofy," but don't throw away the idea of "Birthday Bash" in your honor as a perfect sales event. I know two other marketers who took this concept, and one ended up making six figures from this event. (His was a 40th Birthday Bash!)

I also tied my event into a charity: The Make-A-Wish Foundation®. I worked with the central Florida chapter and they were extremely accommodating, instead of trying to contact national headquarters.

Hurry! Only 322 247 22 Seats Remain....This will SELL OUT!

You're cordially invited to...

"Yanik Silver's 30th Birthday Bash"

"I'm Turning The BIG Three-O and I've Decided to Host a Huge Blow Out Birthday Party and Customer Appreciation Event (where I'm footing the bill). Join me January 16th and 17th, 2004 in Warm and Sunny Orlando, Florida For What Will Be THE 'Internet Marketing' Party and Event of the Year!"

Here's Your Chance to Network with the Real "Players" Online, Dramatically Multiply Your New or Existing Internet Business and Discover the 'Hush-Hush' Secrets That Made Me Rich...All for FREE! (I swore up and down I wouldn't do this - but I have so many new moneymaking insights and important discoveries I've never shared anywhere else that I just couldn't keep them all to myself.)

Dear Internet friend,

Wow!! I can't believe I'm turning 30...

It's the big "three-o" for me and I figured that's a darn good reason to throw a HUGE birthday celebration...I'm talking a mega blow out!

This spectacular **Customer Appreciation Celebration and 30th Birthday Bash** is going on January 16th and 17th, 2004 in Orlando, Florida. Trust, me it's going to be the biggest, most valuable, most extraordinary, "JUMBO" 2-day event you've ever attended (and it's **definitely guaranteed to be the most FUN!**).

FIGURE 10.1 A personal invitation to fun and business

Here's the paragraph describing the charity requirement and a second optional (fun) gag gift contest (see Figure 10.2 on page 130).

It was pretty cool that we were able to raise $25,000 for Make-A-Wish® and really make a difference in a lot of kids' lives.

How Registration Works
PLEASE READ THIS CAREFULLY

There is one simple requirement for getting into the Birthday Bash:

1. There is a $50 charitable donation required to attend. The whole $50 will go to Make-a-Wish® of Central and Northern Florida. Your donation will help grant the wishes of children with life-threatening medical conditions. I've personally donated thousands and thousands of dollars to the Make-a-Wish Foundation® and I'm hoping that we'll be able to grant at least two or three wishes with the amount we raise. The $50 donation is paid now and is non-refundable to hold your spot—but there is no fee for the event.

The event is going on at Disney's Coronado Spring Resorts. We have negotiated a special rate of only $131/night with the hotel for seminar attendees (During prime vacation time this is a real steal). Information for registering will be given to you (only) when you have confirmed seminar registration. Let me assure you, Disney's Coronado Spring Resorts is a great resort that you'll really enjoy! It's close to all the Disney parks and other attractions.

And then there's also a second OPTIONAL admission requirement that gets you entered into a fabulous contest!

2. (OPTIONAL) A gag gift for me. Show up with some sort of silly or funny gag gift for me and you'll be entered into a contest for the "best gag gift." The winner will be decided by an attendee vote. You might want to give this gift a bit of thought because the winner will receive either a half-day consultation with me (that's $2,000 value) or $500 in cash. And the runner-up will get their choice of one of our best-selling products or $200 in cash.

FIGURE 10.2 Think of additional ways to "bake-in" giving and fun for any venture

Then, as far as the gag-gift contest went, that got pretty out of control during the event. I loved it! We got piles and piles of gifts. Some were definitely a bit off-kilter. One guy from the United Kingdom thought it was a stag party and handed me a ream of porn magazines. Another guy brought over some endangered animal pelt. Someone else gave me a family heirloom passed down through generations.

I mean, you name it—I got it. Fart machines, dancing birthday bears, a giant sack of fake money (I like that one), a picture of me with Al Gore saying I invented the internet, a blank book "written" by me called Everything I Know about the Internet, and so on. We even had a beagle come out and bark "Happy Birthday" to me.

I bring all this up because it's all part of the birthday party theme. If you are going to do a theme, go for it all the way! We had confetti on the tables, balloons all over the seminar room, banners, etc. We even brought out cake (yes, very thin slices) for everyone and Mickey Mouse came out to lead the crowd in singing "Happy Birthday."

All these little touches made it a lot of fun for everyone attending, even if each speaker was selling something. The whole attitude of most of the people there was that they've never had such a great time and learned so much.

UNDERGROUND® ONLINE SEMINAR REDUX

OK, let me showcase another theme I've mentioned before: Underground® Online Seminar.

I've already shared the thinking behind the Underground and how it was meant to be a complete, 180-degree shift from any other internet event since every speaker is a "real-world" doer and not someone who sells "How to Get Rich Online" as their main business. So at a brainstorming meeting with my own MasterMind group, the theme became a spy theme.

I really tried to play up the theme in every communication and "touch" a prospect has from me relating to the Underground. It's evolved a bit since the very first event, and I'll share with you some interesting examples along to way to show how.

Figure 10.3 features one of the first direct mail pieces that went out.

FIGURE 10.3 Spy-themed direct mail piece promoting the Underground® seminar

Instead of having speakers or presenters, we had "Rogue Agents" with their front and spy profiles displayed like they were "wanted." I gave each speaker a distinct agent name. See Figure 10.4.

I truly tied to tie everything into a full spy experience. The event was (and still is) held in Washington, DC, because that's the spy capital of the world. And once attendees got to the event, they were immersed in the world of the Underground.

We had two checkpoints set up for participants to sign their non-disclosure agreement (called the "Cone of Silence," from the TV show *Get Smart*—which nobody picked up on!), and then they were handed their spy briefcase.

Now, inside the briefcase was the attendee manual, a T-shirt ("Official Underground Agent"), and official Underground sunglasses.

The theme continued throughout the event, with the VIP dinner being held at the Spy Museum in Washington, DC. We had a private dinner there and really played it up. There were two Russian border patrol guards checking for passwords at the entry. Boris and Natasha showed up for a little entertainment. And finally, the whole group went on a private tour of the Spy Museum.

For the following year's Underground® II, I went even further.

This time I used a specific spy—Austin Powers—instead of a combination of all spy themes. I wanted to keep it different enough that people who attended the first seminar would still be surprised and

FIGURE 10.4 Rogue agent profile

excited with the second. Underground® II sold out even faster than the first one, and we added 100 more seats.

And going with the movie theme, here's a little preview movie poster I had created before we announced the event. See Figure 10.5.

I really got into character for this one. Actually, it wasn't hard because I love Austin Powers and that was one of my favorite Halloween costumes ever.

I really decided to up the ante a lot and bring in professional entertainment for the VIP dinner. I hired an improv troupe from Canada who were all "Second City" alum. They were awesome! We called it a "Mystery Spy Whodunit" dinner, and everyone was roaring in their seats, especially when I was killed off. Somebody started yelling, "Search the dead guy for drink tickets!"

I decided to go full tilt and hire a celebrity tied to the theme, so I booked "Mini Me," aka Verne Troyer, from the Austin Powers movies. Surprisingly, it's not as much as you'd think to book a celebrity (depending on their status), and it can really add a lot to your events.

Having a celebrity there not only gives you excitement but provides additional reason to contact your customers.

Then, the next year for Underground® III, I kept up the theme, but this time it was a "Mission Profitable" theme and I brought in Peter Graves from the original *Mission Impossible* TV series. And when I did the Underground® UK, we had a James Bond theme with the prize being an Aston Martin race day experience.

COUNT YANIK

You don't need to rack your brain for a theme or something to add fun into your business. A calendar of holidays and events is full of perfect excuses for fun.

A few Halloweens ago, I released my "Ultimate At-Home Internet Copywriting Course" (www.ultimatecopyworkshop.com).

FIGURE 10.5 Pouring on the fun and character with a movie-poster spy

I planned the launch during Halloween and wanted to create a bit of a stir in the internet marketing community—try to get some people talking about what I was doing. So my idea was to become "Count Yanik." You see, the previous Halloween I dressed up as "The Count" from *Sesame Street*. Missy said I was the most annoying guest at the party because I went around counting everything.

"One, two, three beer bottles . . . Ahhhhh . . . Ahhhh!"

"One, two, three, four, five hot dogs. . . Ahhhhh . . . Ahhhh!"

OK, so maybe I was annoying, but I had fun.

Regardless, I had one good photo of me in my purple makeup, monocle, and black cape. That became a key part of my campaign. I sent our subscribers to this page with a message from the "Count": www. UltimateCopywritingWorkshop.com/count/.

It's a flash animation file I had created where you see a purple bat fly into the screen and turn into a talking "Count Yanik." Then I turn back into a bat and fly out of the screen. I paid $150 to have this created at Rent-a-Coder, which has enjoyed so much success it is now called vWorker (www.vworker.com)—and it's super cheap!

Then, on the landing page, there's more Halloween theme. I really got into it with the "bloody" text. See Figure 10.6.

FIGURE 10.6 Landing page for Count Yanik

DOES ALL THIS "FUN" STUFF ACTUALLY TRANSLATE TO SALES?

This event sold over six figures' worth of my copywriting course in the first week on the market. Actually, more specifically, 114 packages sold for a total of $145,350.00. So this stuff works!

Now there are a couple big points I really want to make sure you get before I go on with other examples:

1. Make your marketing fun and have people wonder: What is this guy/gal up to next? Fact is, most of your prospects and customers probably lead fairly normal and mundane lives. If you can give them something to get excited about, or even live a little bit through what you do, you'll have hooked them in.

2. This is critical! Don't make your theme or "fun" idea take away from the sales message. Big advertisers do this all the time and waste all their money. They try to use humor or something clever in their advertising, but have no salesmanship. The fun or theme aspect of your promotion cannot stand on its own without the fundamentals of direct response (e.g., a compelling offer, deadline, headlines, benefits, etc.). Bottom line: Don't confuse this with being cute or clever and not actually selling. There is a big, BIG difference.

3. "Reason why" copy works perfectly for most of the events or themes you create. As you know, most retailers will use some sort of event, like Presidents Day, for a sale. Well, that's a pretty weak reason why, but most people will accept just about any excuse for a special deal. However, when you combine it with real, meaningful "reason why" copy, it works even better, even if the reason is a bit contrived. For example, I did a "Save Yanik's Marriage" sale when I needed to clean out our stockroom because Missy was pissed off at me.

Using this psychological hot button can massively increase your marketing success.

Max Sackheim, famous for the long-running ad, "Do You Make These Mistakes in English?" and originator of the book-of-the-month concept, says this: "Whenever you make a claim or special offer in your advertising, come up with an honest reason why, and then state it sincerely. You'll sell many more products this way."

ADDING MORE FUN TO A REGULAR BUSINESS

I'm always interested in what companies do to add more fun to their business. Certainly, booking a hotel room usually isn't the most exciting thing in the world (well, I guess it can be if you're going to a cool resort), but otherwise a room is pretty much a room. I'm a big fan of the W Hotels.

A recent promo I got from them was promoting a "Sleep Away Camp" theme. Smart. The copy ties into this theme, from the s'mores to bug juice—good stuff and a little inspiration for you to think up something fun for your customers. Personally, I think simply delivering a straightforward product or service will only get you so far. The companies that will excel are the ones that deliver true experiences and entertainment for their customers. People are bored. People are busy. People are jaded. You need something to break through all of that.

CREATING MORE FUN AWAY FROM BUSINESS

OK, now let's switch gears and talk about your personal life. I know for many entrepreneurs (including me), the default mode is work. There are always too many projects and too many to-dos left undone. That's why I firmly believe you need to have something else scheduled and on the calendar.

Think back to when you were a kid and what activities or interests got you really jazzed and excited. Somehow, as adults, many of us have lost that sense of fun and inspiration. What did you like to do? For me, it was playing sports, drawing, and making people laugh. That's why I still play ice hockey and beach volleyball, why I've taken art classes and stand-up comedy classes. I make sure to incorporate what gives me enjoyment into my life by actually making it a priority.

How many times have you heard yourself saying, "I'd love to (insert your desire here) BUT I can't, because I'm too busy." That's total bull. What you're really saying is: "That activity does not have enough priority in my life." Or, "I feel guilt around having fun."

Don't just settle for enjoying life when you squeeze it in between your business. Here's a great quote from Jim Loehr and Tony Schwartz, authors of *The New York Times* bestseller, *The Power of Full Engagement*: ". . . the richer and deeper the source of emotional recovery, the more we refill our reserves and the more resilient we become."

Put fun activities, rewarding experiences, and exceptional adventures on your calendar and protect them like you would any "real" appointment.

CREATING YOUR ULTIMATE BIG LIFE LIST

I've always been a fan of lists and I know many other successful people share this notion. What better list can you create than a list for your most memorable and exciting life? I call this my "Ultimate Big Life List."

This is pretty easy and encompasses everything I want to do, have, or become before I die. The hard part is sitting down and just jotting down the list, but before you get there, let me start with my own list.

On my InternetLifestyle.com blog, I have posted in the right sidebar, under "Yanik's Big List," a running list of the experiences I want to achieve, but my personal BIG list extends beyond that, as I mentioned before.

Here are a few examples from my list (aside from what I published on my blog):

▶ Host *Saturday Night Live*
▶ Fly my own plane
▶ Play in an NHL hockey game

- Stand-up comedy at a club
- ~~Lunch with Sir Richard Branson~~
- Dance the Hakka with the All Blacks in New Zealand
- Taste a 100-year-old Bordeaux
- Dance all night in Ibiza
- Donate over $10,000,000 to meaningful charities in my lifetime
- Visit the place I was born in: Russia
- Blow off school with Zak and Zoe once a year as a surprise father-son-daughter adventure
- Own a fully restored MGA
- My name engraved on the Stanley Cup as an owner of the Washington Capitals
- Start my own profitable liquor brand
- Create a charitable foundation to educate a million young entrepreneur startups
- Own a vineyard and produce award-winning wines
- ~~Be a semi-professional beach volleyball player~~
- ~~Financial independence~~
- ~~Drive a race car at over 200 mph~~
- Be part of an IPO as an insider
- Participate in the Olympics
- Become a *New York Times* bestselling author
- Write a bestselling children's book on success
- Live to be a vibrant and healthy 127 years old

Most of my own BIG list is centered around "DO," but that's just me. Yours is unique to you. Right now, my list spans over 100 items, and it keeps growing. I believe in one afternoon you could get at least 25 to 50 items on your own list . The first few are easy, but then you really have to dig into what would make you happy.

- What excited you as a kid?
- What have you always wanted to do?
- What have you always wanted to be?

▸ What have you always wanted to see?

▸ What have you always wanted to have?

Just don't get bogged down in what other people will think. Don't put something on your list that doesn't excite you or put it there because you think you're supposed to. Hey, if you don't want to save the whales, screw 'em. Don't put it on your list.

If you're stuck for what to put on your own list I have a bunch of idea starters for you at www.MaverickBusinessInsider.com/lifelist—Everything from your top five adventures and experiences, to people you want to meet, and surprises you want to do for your family.

Keep thinking without putting conditions or restrictions on your list. It doesn't matter if you think it's dumb, or couldn't really happen, or think others will laugh at you. So what? Go with your heart and just get it down. There's no harm in writing it down even if it doesn't happen—that's how some of my improbable ones have been accomplished—but I'll tell you about those in a moment as we move on to how you start having fun and checking off items.

HOW DO YOU GET YOUR BIG LIST COMPLETED?

Write it down. Yes, writing it down is the first step, and I absolutely guarantee you if you did nothing else but write 50 to 100 items in your BIG list you'd be surprised at how many actually got done after one year without you ever looking at them again. I don't look at my Big list every day—it's not necessary, but I do certain things to make sure I can check them off.

Fact is, as I was writing this section, I went back over my own list again and was amazed to see that two things on my list were in the process of getting accomplished in the next three weeks (as of this writing). One was kiteboarding at Necker Island and, at the same time, lunch with Sir Richard Branson. I'm heading to Necker Island in a few weeks and I'll definitely try kiteboarding on the island. Plus, I'll be there with Sir Richard for several days, so lunch is inevitable. Pretty cool!

Just the mere fact of writing it down and releasing it to the Universe gives you an advantage that circumstances might be set into motion and start conspiring to work for you. (Hey, that's my belief, anyway!)

For instance, I've previously written down I wanted to be a semi-pro beach volleyball player. I really didn't think it would happen, but I figured it wouldn't hurt to write it down. Well, now I'd technically be considered a pro (even though my wife, Missy, might say differently).

It started when I was instant-messaging with my friend, AVP (Association of Volleyball Profssionals) pro Albert Hannemann (Al-B), and he was telling me his doubles volleyball partner just bailed on him at the last minute for the final tournament of the 2007 season in Cincinnati. I was joking around with Al-B that we should play together in the tournament, since he couldn't find anyone else. HA! Yeah, right— like he needs a 5'-8", partly-out-of-shape partner.

Imagine my surprise when he said, "Yes!"

Al-B and I have been friends from the Volleyball vacations trips (VolleyballVacation.com) he runs, and I've given him some advice on marketing and promotion. I know my skill level, and it's not pro. I hadn't played more than three times that entire summer, and I was making some really stupid mistakes on easy serves.

We got knocked out in the first qualifying match, 18–21 and 19–21 (ugh!). I guess it could have been much worse, but I really thought we should have won that match. Though, in consolation, I did get three or four service aces, a couple big digs, and a few kills out there.

The promoter from the AVP Cincinnati event loved our story about coming together on IM and joining up for this tournament. He suggested I make a $1,000 donation to buy tickets for local Special Olympics athletes to come watch the tournament. It was a great idea and that's exactly what I did. Actually Al-B and I both share the same views about giving back. He runs the DIG for Kids charity (www.Dig4Kids.org) and I promised I'd support that this year. In fact, we made a deal for next year (if it happens again) that I'll make it really fun and do something like donating $100 for every point we score, $250 for every dig I make, and something crazy like $5,000 for every block I make. Hopefully, I'll get to redeem myself in another tournament.

Now since I not only got volleyball pro checked off, I decided to add a few more sports items to the list on the plane ride home, including "Get my name engraved on the Stanley Cup." Hey—why not?

Here's another one that's interesting. Do I really think I'll be in the Olympics? I dunno. Probably not—but there's a tiny shot. Who knows? My publicist mentioned to me the other day he was friends with the former publicist for the U.S. Bobsled and Skeleton Federation. I don't know how many people are waiting in line to go 80 mph headfirst down an icy track, so who knows if I'd get a tryout. Maybe—maybe not. But if I didn't throw it out there to the Universe and write it down, I know I wouldn't hear the faint knocking on the door of opportunity.

Schedule it. This is where a lot of people fall down, and it might sound a bit too rigid for busy entrepreneurs, but unless you schedule your fun (most of the time), it won't happen. It sounds a bit counterintuitive, doesn't it? Fun should be spontaneous and free? Well, guess what? If you stick to your typical schedule, it'll never happen, because your work will keep expanding to the allotted time you give it. You can always do one more work item and your inbox is never going to be empty.

Think about your vacation for a moment. That's scheduled and it happens precisely because it is scheduled. The more fun you schedule into your life, the more you'll get. What about when you were a kid? Most of us had mandatory fun built into our days with recess, right?

WHY ISN'T THERE RECESS FOR ENTREPRENEURS?

Now, you probably won't go and play dodge ball this afternoon, but you can have your own recess if you do something about it yourself. Some of my most memorable fun times have been things I've gone after and not waited to have them fall into my lap.

This might sound a little "type A" (which I'm definitely not), but you have to put fun activities on your calendar or else your fun and entertainment by default becomes vegging in front of the TV or working more. Of course, it's great to be spontaneous, but unless you are completely free of responsibilities, you'll need to make plans. And making plans could be as simple as inviting friends over for a night of games or as wild as running with the bulls in Spain.

Recruit Others

It's tough to get everything on your BIG list done yourself, especially if you're really stretched for time. That's why it's important to share your BIG Life List with others who can help you.

But there's a caveat here. I'd be selective of who I share with. You don't want a negative, dream-stealing vampire to stick their fangs into your life list. But when you find positive, excited individuals, ask them what's on their own "Life To-Do" list and see if you don't have a resource or a step in the right direction you can give them. And those same successful people have their own connections and people they know who might get you where you want to be.

Fact is, life is going to pass with or without you taking charge (just like in business). It's the people who are proactive and put fun activities on their calendars who live life to the fullest. I have a saying: "You can't control how you'll die but you can control how you live." It's the difference between being a spectator and being a participant.

SHUTTING DOWN YOUR EXCUSES

At this point, a little voice inside your head might be whispering (or shouting) about all the reasons you can't do this kind of fun stuff in your life. These excuses will sap the spirit and energy out of your life. As entrepreneurs, we're naturally inclined to create, so let's smash these final excuses to create what you really want in your life and business.

It's too easy for all of us to simply believe we'll "get around to it," or "someday" we'll have more fun, but one excuse or another comes up. Try these on for size:

Maverick Library

Here are some good books that might help get you going:

- *Die Happy: 499 Things Every Guy's Gotta Do While He Still Can*, Tim and Michael Burke (St. Martin's Griffin, 2006)
- *1,000 Places to See Before You Die: A Traveler's Life List*, Patricia Schultz (Workman Publishing Company, 2003)
- *No Opportunity Wasted*, Phil Keoghan, host of *The Amazing Race* and Warren Berger (Rodale Books, 2006)
- *101 Things to Do Before You Die*, Richard Horne (Bloomsbury USA, 2005)

And here are some sites to inspire you:

- www.43things.com
- www.ReaperList.com
- www.InternetLifestyle.com—my blog
- www.tedstake.com/2006/01/06/my-101-list-the-story—Internet pioneer, former AOL executive, and owner of the Washington Capitals, Ted Leonis shares his own "101" list. This list was written after Ted went through the harrowing experience of a near-crash of his plane.
- www.noopportunitywasted.com—Phil Keoghan, the host of TV's *The Amazing Race*, created his original list after a near-death experience at the age of 19 while scuba diving.
- www.johngoddard.info/life_list.htm—John Goddard, one of the biggest adventurers and greatest goal setters in the world.

I Don't Have Time to Do This Stuff

When I hear people say they don't have time for something, it really means that item is not a priority for them. The excuse of "I don't have time" is commonly accepted, but if you stop and think about it, we all have the same 24 hours in a day. It's up to you to decide what your priorities are. And if a priority is living a full, rich life with incredible experiences and adventures, then you'll create the time and schedule items from your BIG list.

Think about where you might be spending time now, and make the conscious decision whether that's what you want to do, or would you rather be doing something from your BIG list. Or what are you doing now that you could pay someone else to do? I don't cut my own lawn, clean my house, wash my car, drop off my dry cleaning, buy stamps, or a dozen other simple activities. Why? Because I know I can easily pay someone to do this and it frees me up to either create additional revenue streams or enjoy my life.

I Can't Leave My Business Long Enough to Do This

A close cousin to not having enough time is believing you can't get away from your business long enough to knock off any of the fun items on your list. You can get a lot done in just a few days, and your company will not fall apart without you. If you cannot leave your office for a few days without things getting off track, you have some serious system issues that need to be worked on. (Leaving will actually expose them to you.) Most times, if people are left to fend for themselves without the "big boss" approving everything, things will still get done correctly. Maybe not quite the way you would do it, but the end result would be close enough, and you'd have the freedom to enjoy your life.

In fact, I think freedom is the operative keyword for entrepreneurs, and unless we exercise that freedom by stepping away from the office, it slowly collapses. We become nothing more than highly paid servants to our businesses. You might believe you're indispensable, but nearly everyone (including you) is replaceable. It's important to step back and see if you are truly operating on activities in your business that are core competencies and unique abilities where you excel.

You've probably heard of the Pareto principle, or 80/20 rule. It states that approximately 20 percent of your activities produce 80 percent of the results. Conversely, 80 percent of your activities create 20 percent of the results. So if you focus on the critical few activities that produce 80 percent of the results, this will free up your time to do even more outside of work.

My Friends/Family/Dog Will Think I'm Crazy

So what? Maybe they will, but who cares? My wife and her family think I'm pretty nuts, but I don't mind. I realized I'm wired differently and that's OK. Typically, my wife, Missy, won't come on my adventures, and that's fine because she has a different idea of vacations than I do. We do things apart and we do things together.

Now, on the other hand, my stepmother is a huge worrier and doesn't want to know when I go jump out of airplanes or go Baja racing. She's OK if I tell her after the fact, when I'm home safe and sound. And that's fine, too. The only thing that's not fine is the people who attempt to reel you in because they know better or think they're helping. They might say, "Don't you care about your family?" or "Aren't you getting too old for this kind of thing?" or my favorite, "You can't always get what you want."

These negative people are simply replaying the tapes spinning in their heads. They can keep their boring and dull existence—I'd rather create the kind of memories that last forever and give me something more interesting to talk about than the local football team or the weather.

X-Factor 11

CREATE THE IMPACT

THE MAVERICK METHOD OF GIVING MORE

Nearly all the successful people I know give exponentially more than they take. There's a special kind of satisfaction that comes from helping and serving others. Entrepreneurs are some of the most generous and giving individuals I've been fortunate enough to associate with.

A lot of people talk about how they want to donate some huge sum of money to a charity or their church, but then never get around to it because they feel like they don't have enough right now, or it's not the right time. Frankly, I think it's because it is not a systematic, regimented giving plan. If you would have told me a few years ago I'd regularly be giving $10,000, $15,000, and $20,000 checks to charities, I would have thought you were crazy because I could use that extra money myself for something. But when it becomes just a way you operate, it's much easier to start writing those checks with big zeros behind them. My dad thinks I'm nuts when I tell him how much I donate, but I'm more than pleased with my decision.

WHERE I FOUND THIS

One of the first times I heard about this was from the late Foster Hibbard (an interview with him is featured at John Harricharan's site, www.insight2000.com/prosperity.html), who worked with Napoleon Hill. Foster talked about setting up a "giving account" and a "wealth account." The setup was simple. You would take a fixed percentage of all money that comes in to you (e.g., 5 percent, 10 percent, etc.) and put that amount into both accounts each time you received it. I only do this monthly, but this follows the "pay yourself first" philosophy of getting rich, also. So each month, 5 percent gets paid off the top, no matter what, to me (for investments and buying assets, not toys) and 5 percent gets paid to a charity of my choice. (Dan Kennedy worked with Foster Hibbard and has a great distillation of this and his own wealth-building philosophy in his book, *No BS Wealth Attraction for Entrepreneurs*.)

Fact is, I could see significant jumps in my own income once I started this 5 percent charitable giving. Some of the wealthiest and most successful people of all time discovered this secret. It's been said that Rockefeller walked around every day with a roll of dimes and gave them away. Carnegie was one of the biggest philanthropists, building public libraries. Many people talk about the "filthy rich" or how greedy rich people are—I've found just the opposite. Most of the truly wealthy and successful individuals are some of the biggest and most generous contributors around.

One perfect example I know is one of my mentors, Frank McKinney, who I introduced to you earlier. *The Wall Street Journal* refers to him as "The Daredevil Developer and Real Estate Rock Czar." Frank builds these mega, multimillion-dollar mansions in Florida on speculation (meaning no buyer before he builds it). And the guy plays just as hard for charity. He founded the Caring House Project Foundation (www. frank-mckinney.com/caring_project.aspx) to build self-sustaining housing and communities for the desperately poor. (I've got a special bonus transcript with Frank of an interview we did together at the end of this chapter.)

YOU CANNOT OUTGIVE THE UNIVERSE

If that statement is true, then anything you give out comes back to you in kind, multiple times. Meaning, from a pragmatic standpoint, you could look at this really as a return on "charitable investment." But that's almost too logical. There's an incredible feeling from knowing one check you wrote sustained an entire village of entrepreneurial upstarts, like when we donate to Village Enterprise Fund (villageef. org). Or when you get a handwritten note from one of the charities you support talking about how surprised they were to get a $15,000 check out of the blue, and what kind of help that means to their program.

Personally, I do due diligence on the charity I'm going to support for that particular month, and then I write the check without expectation of what is going to happen with the money.

TIME, TALENT, AND TREASURE

One of our Maverick1000 members, Mike Lally, has a saying that I love, and that's "You can give time, talent, or treasure." So perhaps if you're short on finances, give some of your time away, or talent. Quite frankly, for years now we pretty much only donated money (treasure) since that's what I had the most abundance of. Today, with the Young Entrepreneur sessions we run on Maverick trips and virtual mentorship, we have the opportunity to actively engage and give forward. Previously I would donate to a lot of different charitable organizations, but now I'm pretty much focused on my passion for young entrepreneurship (www.3percentforward.org is where I'll be starting a movement on this).

MAKING A DIFFERENCE BY ENGAGING YOUR PASSION

At a recent Summit Series event in Aspen, I got the chance to meet Ethan Zohn. If you watched *Survivor*, you might remember him as the $1,000,000 winner. Ethan was a professional soccer player in Zimbabwe before appearing on *Survivor*. He witnessed firsthand the ravages AIDS had on the African people and wanted to do something, but didn't know what. After winning *Survivor*, he had the means and a bit of fame to create an educational program with professional soccer players educating children and teens about AIDS through experiential learning called Grass Roots Soccer.

In Africa, soccer players are some of the biggest heroes for the kids growing up and this makes for a perfect vehicle for spreading awareness and educating. Ethan's nonprofit has impacted more than 220,000 kids and is growing. With the 2010 World Cup in South Africa, his charity was selected to be engaged in bigger outreach programs throughout the continent.

He took his passion (soccer) and turned it into something that made (and is still making) a tremendous difference for a serious epidemic.

REAL-TIME FUNDRAISING

I've got to tip my hat to my friend and Maverick member, Chris Zavadowski. He did a great job really exceeding his goals with a fundraising effort for Charity Water. He put together a cool webinar I was on with a few internet experts sharing what they're doing now, and throughout the event he asked people to post in Twitter or Facebook about the donation page (www.mycharitywater.org/helpavillage).

He ended up raising more than $20,000 and significantly blowing past his initial goals. And a lot of it was similar to the old telethon models. Charity Water has a great tool where you can see in real-time what the donation amount is. This type of social proof causes others to donate or previous donors to re-commit and donate more to reach the next goal.

BUY ONE, GIVE ONE

I've really been inspired lately by TOMS shoes with their simple giving model. When you buy a pair of shoes for yourself, they donate a pair to a child in need. Easy to understand and truly impactful. In just three years they've already donated 150,000 pairs of shoes.

In Aspen, I also had the chance to meet Lauren and Ellen from FEED. I've mentioned them before, but not the story behind FEED. Lauren Bush was a student at Princeton University when she saw the United Nations World Hunger program was looking for a student spokesperson. She applied and went to work firsthand with a program that delivered meals to impoverished children in third-world countries. From that on-the-ground experience she was forever changed and wanted to make an impact. She had the idea of combining some of her fashion contacts she made as a model with this idea of charitable giving.

Her idea was simple but profound. Create a fashionable bag that people would want and that also feeds x amount of children per year, hence the name FEED bag. The only problem was the United Nations is not an entrepreneurial venture. They didn't get the concept of selling at retail to donate a percentage for a specific cause. Lauren had a deal set up with Amazon.com, but they needed a vendor name for the application, so she enlisted Ellen from the United Nations, a kindred spirit, to create a company on the fly for this.

From that small beginning, the FEED bag then got sold in Whole Foods and has ended up raising more than $2.4 million for the hunger program, enough to cover the entire Rwandan program by itself.

To me I find even more exciting than giving a percentage is having a tangible result instead of a percentage charitable donation. With the FEED bag you know for one bag bought you've fed ten children. This is a BIG idea!

This tangible and specific charity by-product of a sale got me thinking. In fact, in our "Painted Picture," I reference this. We've already started this with Maverick1000, where we donate to Village Enterprise

Fund and fund three microbusinesses for every member who joins. And we want to do this even more with a specific product tied into a specific charitable action.

I own a few pairs of Pact underwear. They give away 10 percent of their sales to different causes and many times have special limited-edition underwear to support specific causes. Cool social entrepreneurs for sure!

What I want to point out is their packaging is in total alignment with their social good. You have to think about your "DNA" all the way through your product or service. They are a mail-order underwear company, so using the wrong packaging would send the wrong message. Here's what they say on their outside mailing envelope:

> *Not only do we recommend a daily change of underwear, we also recommend making a daily change in our world. This 100 percent compostable package is here to help with both. Just like you toss your underwear in with your dirty clothes, you can literally toss this bag in with your dirt. Even the mailing label and adhesive will decompose in less than 45 days.*

Now that is cool and in total alignment with their company values.

OK, here's the bonus interview transcript I promised with Frank McKinney:

FRANK MCKINNEY INTERVIEW: EXTREME SUCCESS SECRETS

YANIK: Frank is truly an American original. He's a real estate artist, two-time international bestselling author, and a visionary who sees opportunities and creates real estate markets where none existed before.

At the age of 18, with $50 in his pocket, without the benefit of higher education, Frank left his native Indiana for Florida in search of his highest calling. Today, Frank builds eight-figure, nine-figure, even ten-figure oceanfront spec homes, meaning that there is no buyer lined up before he starts building it.

Some of you may have seen Frank featured on *20/20*, on *Oprah*, on the cover of *USAToday*, or even in *The Wall Street Journal*, where they referred to him as the "Daredevil Developer and Real Estate Rock Star."

There's so much more about Frank that we could spend the whole hour talking about all the different things that he's done. Another big part of Frank's life that I know we're going to get into—because it's one of the reasons we're doing this call—is his Caring House Foundation charity that he has done a whole lot with serving people who are in underprivileged areas, building housing for them.

I'm proud to say that I've helped sponsor that. It's such a good cause. We'll be talking about that for sure.

Frank, is there anything that I left off that you want to fill in a few gaps on?

FRANK: No. First, just a big huge thank you to you, Yanik, for not only what you've done with your students in teaching people to live a full and balanced life, to succeed in what I call "the business of life." You are highly regarded out there. A lot of people speak extremely highly of you. I don't tend to get involved with anybody unless they check out okay. Your reputation is stellar, not to mention your recent generosity through our Caring House Project Foundation.

I've been looking forward to this because everybody tells me how great your calls are. We haven't done one together so I'm jazzed to share the better part of an hour.

I think, while we're going through this, a good thing for folks to do while they're listening is to pull up Frank-McKinney.com, if that's all right, Yanik.

YANIK: Absolutely.

FRANK: If you pull up the home page, Frank-McKinney.com, as Yanik and I are bantering back and forth, you can see some of the exciting for-profit projects that we're doing. As Yanik referenced, we're building the world's largest and most expensive spec home at $135 million. Simultaneously, we're building the largest certified green, environmentally friendly home at $30 million, which is actually about 15 times more expensive than any house built to green standards.

There's a little bit about the books we've written; but most importantly, on that homepage, you can click and learn more about this upcoming experience we're going to be hosting down here in Florida that Yanik is going to co-host with me.

YANIK: Yes, I'm very much looking forward to that. We'll definitely get into that.

From $50 in your pocket to building $135 million spec homes, that's a long journey. I hope to get a little bit of the Frank McKinney insight out of you. I've read your book, *Make It Big!*, which I thought was great—then with a subtitle of *49 Secrets for Building a Life of Extreme Success.* I definitely suggest anyone to go out and get it.

You also have one just on real estate. The name escapes me, I'm sorry to say.

FRANK: *Frank McKinney's Maverick Approach to Real Estate Success.*

YANIK: Great! I haven't read that one, but if it's anything like the other one, it's full of great insight as well. Take us from that kid in Indiana, leaving with $50 in his pocket, to now building houses and selling multimillion-dollar mansions...

FRANK: Sure.

YANIK: Let's start with the one that I pulled out of your book: how to recognize your highest calling and passion early on. A lot of people have this problem of feeling bored, feeling that they're not involved in their full capacity. If you find your highest calling and your passion— correct me if I'm wrong, but—it doesn't seem like work anymore.

FRANK: You're right. Most people can search an entire lifetime to determine what their professional highest calling is. I believe we both—you and I and everybody listening—have both a professional and a spiritual highest calling. The beauty, the "ah-ha!" nirvana moment takes places when you're able to put those two together and dovetail professional with spiritual highest calling.

When we're seeking, we kind of need to find that professional one first, because spiritual highest calling doesn't pay too well. It makes a huge impact with human capital, but as far as financial capital, there isn't a whole lot there.

What I did is, as a juvenile delinquent, high-school dropout who went from high school to high school, I ended up graduating from my fourth high school in four years with a 1.8 grade point average. I came to Florida with that $50 bill in my pocket, Yanik, seeking my highest calling. I didn't know I was seeking it at the time.

Of course, at 18 years old, you don't know much. I began to, by the process of elimination, determine what it was that I didn't want to be any longer. That's a lot easier than determining what you do want to be. What don't you want to be, Frank?

I didn't want to be a troublemaker. I didn't want to be the cause for my mother to turn prematurely grey. I didn't want to be a drain on society. I didn't want to constantly be in trouble, constantly looking over my shoulder, digging myself out of a ditch.

I started to eliminate one by one the self-defeating characteristics that I think we all have, everybody at different levels. Clean the plate. I'm a firm believer that there are only a handful of times in our lifetime that we can take the imaginary eraser, turn around and look at the imaginary chalkboard, and erase the past: when we come out of high school, when we come out of college, when we get our first job, when we get married, and when we have kids.

That's it! In my opinion, those are the do-overs. I came out of high school, took out that eraser, and said, "I'm going to leave these damaging characteristics, the less-than-disciplined characteristics behind. I'm going to go to Florida and seek my highest calling."

YANIK: Frank, let me stop you for one quick second. I'm curious about this. You said there are times when do-overs can occur. So someone couldn't just stop tomorrow and say this is my list of what I don't want to do?

FRANK: Those are your built-in do-overs. Those are the five opportunities that you've got to take it out. Those are times that I want to make sure—everybody goes through those five—most everybody goes through those five phases. Recognize those.

If you're a parent listening and you have a troubled teen, I'm less worried about the troubled teen as I am about the parent freaking out about the troubled teen. If you've given them that good foundation, you can encourage them by saying, "Johnny, you've got an opportunity coming out of high school to get rid of that bad behavior."

Those are the automatic ones; those are the built-in mulligans, if you're a golfer. You've got five of them. Absolutely, after a call like today's, you realize that, "Wow! I've got the power to grab an eraser and turn around and begin, one by one—it doesn't happen overnight—erasing the oversleeping, and overeating, and drug use, and womanizing, and gambling."

All these things that make us ordinary people.

I have a favorite saying in my first book. "To live an extraordinary life, you must resist an ordinary approach."

YANIK: Yes, that's definitely one of the things I want to get into.

FRANK: To live an extraordinary life, you must resist an ordinary approach. What's ordinary? Some of those vices I just referenced. Some of them aren't even vices; they're just bad habits.

I wanted to get rid of all of those and seek my highest calling. When I wrote my book, obviously, I recognized what I was doing back at 18 was seeking a highest calling.

There are five criteria, and I want to go through them very quickly, that need to be considered if you're thinking that internet business-building or real estate construction, or being a Tupperware manufacturer—it doesn't matter—five criteria that need to be met for something to be considered the highest calling.

The first one is it's got to involve your heart. It's got to be something that you find emotionally fulfilling. Just put that on the piece of paper: heart involved; emotionally fulfilling.

Next, if the heart's involved, the head needs to get involved. It's got be something that you've got potential for. For example, I want to be an opera singer, but I can't carry a tune. Just cross it off the list; it's not going to happen. I want to be the King of France. I want to be the heir to the throne.

Some people's expectations—and I'm all for dreaming big, but let's be realistic—let's start to cross off some of the things that the head does not have potential for.

Number three is where most people lose and don't stick with it long enough. It's got to be something that you want to do and feel that you can do for a long time. It might change. There's no doubt. You and I have had a few careers. I was a tennis pro, then I wanted to be an actor, and I wanted to be a stunt man. Then all of a sudden, at 22 years old, I latched onto this real estate thing. I realized that for it to be classified as a highest calling, I needed to be willing to put in time. Perhaps a lifetime in pursuing it.

The fourth item is it's got to be something you feel utilizes all your God-given gifts and talents. I don't believe that we're given certain aptitudes for nothing. I'm not a highly educated person. I didn't go to college and I had that 1.8 grade point average. God gifted me with certain aptitudes and I wanted to make sure I was utilizing those. My highest calling utilizes those.

Lastly, most importantly, your highest calling is something that has to make a difference, not only in your life but also in the lives of others.

Five criteria. Page 17 of my [*Make It BIG!: 49 Secrets for Building a Life of Extreme Success*] first chapter. Check them off. If something that you're pursuing out there doesn't meet—or you don't feel it could meet—those five criteria, move on. The worst thing that could happen in one's life is waking up at 45 years old and realizing you haven't done anything. Would have, could have, should have. But didn't.

I found it really easily when I quantified those five criteria, like getting involved in this charity that I started ten years ago. I feel as much passion for what I do in the not-for-profit world as I do in the for-profit world. To be honest with you, I run my charity like a business. The only difference is there is no profit motive, no financial profit motive. I've got a human capital profit motive. It meets my five criteria.

YANIK: Something I should have pointed out is that Frank has successfully won the Badwater Ultramarathon.

FRANK: A 135-mile race across the desert.

YANIK: Through Death Valley.

FRANK: Yep. I didn't win it; I finished it.

YANIK: Finished! Anyone who finishes is a winner in my book.

FRANK: That's the toughest footrace in the world, according to *National Geographic* and the *Discovery* channel. One hundred and thirty-five miles.

YANIK: That's amazing. He runs that for his Caring House Foundation. You know that Frank is one tough, dedicated guy to be able to go through that.

Let's talk about the flip side: finding the passion and the higher calling for the spiritual side. You said we also have that.

FRANK: This gets a little deeper into the conversation. It's something that shouldn't be glossed over, because I have found through my interaction with very, very wealthy people—the average selling price of our houses since 1992 has been $12 million. I have the good fortune of meeting a lot of very successful, ultra-successful people. Over the course of the last 15 years where we've been operating at that price point, I've met my fair share of unhappy billionaires.

In the same span of time, I've met my fair share of very happy homeless people. What's the difference? These people got to the top rung of the corporate ladder; they got there, put their hand on their forehead looking out over the horizon, and said to themselves, "Is this all there is?"

They became extremely depressed with the pursuit of the almighty top rung via the almighty dollar and were left spiritually hollow. They had no reason to get up in the morning other than to go look at their brokerage account or their bank account and count the number of cars in their garage.

Especially the younger we are, we are very impressionable. When I was in my 20s, it was all about the Ferraris and the fancy cars. We think that's the definition of success. It's not when we compare it to those who leave the legacies that we're proud of.

You might like to watch *MTV Cribs* and watch a rapper or somebody who has made their instantaneous fortune. I would check back with a lot of folks in ten years to see if they have that flash-in-the-pan variety of success or the legacy type of success that is generational in nature.

Once I felt—well, I didn't feel; I know—I was being mentored by these billionaires. As I sold them the houses, I got to become friends with them. Since I lost my father in a plane crash in 1992, I have a tendency to latch onto the father figure and learn from them.

I found that the ones who had come in contact with and embraced their spiritual highest calling were the ones that were living the most balanced, fulfilled, and happy lives.

It wasn't just reserved for the wealthy. I did my sister's taxes one year. She had a year where she earned five figures. She had a five-figure income. Two of those figures were separated by a decimal point.

In other words, she earned less than $1000—$989 and some cents. I did her taxes. She was the most fulfilled, happy person because she was over in Tacna, Peru, working at a center for children who actually had to go to work at three and four years old because they have to make ends meet for their families. The center allowed these children to be kids for a day.

There have been countless instances. As a matter of fact, the next book I'm writing is entitled *The Tap*. It's about God tapping each and every one of us on the shoulder and learning how to listen for that spiritual highest calling tap. What are the signs? Unfortunately, most of us don't answer that.

For me, very simply put, I'm a simpleton, an uneducated guy who is in the housing business. Simple. Yes, they're fancy; yes, they're beautiful; yes, it's a spec house. We don't know if we're going to have a buyer or not. At the same time, if you strip it all down, I'm in the housing business.

Why not take what I know, which is the housing business, and provide shelter for those who don't have any? That's as simple as it was back in 1998 when I started my charity. I wanted to live out my childhood dream of being the modern day Robin Hood. I wanted to sell to the rich—not steal from them. I wanted to sell to the rich and I wanted to provide housing to the world's most desperately poor and homeless.

After being in business for myself since 1986, come 1998—12 years later—I was able to finally bring together that professional highest calling with the spiritual highest calling. Not only have I felt more fulfilled, my business has taken off.

It doesn't matter what your religious preference is. I will tell you that there's a passage in the Bible in the Gospel of Luke. I will paraphrase it. To whom much is entrusted, much will be expected. The more that you are entrusted with, the more that will be expected from you.

I take this spiritual highest calling very, very seriously. It's a responsibility. It's a stewardship that needs to be developed.

You might be thinking, "That's easy for Yanik to do because he's a multimillionaire. It's easy for Frank to do because he's wealthy. You guys are set up and you're in a position to take care of those less fortunate."

True, but untrue, in that the three T's reference in the Bible—time, talent, and treasure—Yanik has the treasure to share and he does so very generously. You may not. You listening may not. What about the first T? For Frank, it started with the first T. I started with sharing time.

I used to go around in a beat-up, old Econoline van bringing hot meals to the homeless in the back alleys of the bad neighborhoods of West Palm Beach, Florida. One night a week. That was it. That's all I did. Every Monday night, before *Monday Night Football*, for three years straight, I went out and served meals to the homeless.

It was very fulfilling. It was all I had to give. I didn't have talent. I didn't have, certainly, that much treasure. As I began to develop a talent for fixing up houses, I used to go out and fix up houses in neighborhoods for an elderly shut-in woman who was an invalid and couldn't come out and paint her front porch. It was little things like that.

Then, I realized that was good. I developed my talent. Then I started to make a little money and we moved onto the third and final T, which is sharing our treasure.

That, to me, is pursuing one's spiritual highest calling. You would be amazed. Give and it will be given back tenfold, they say. I haven't seen the tenfold return but I'll take "give and it will be given back to you even half that." Fivefold. You will be amazed at what happens in your professional life once you tap into your spiritual highest calling.

YANIK: That's interesting because I've started publicly sharing what I've been doing for a long time privately. We give away 10 percent of all our gross income to different charities. I've made tremendous income jumps just when I started doing that. I didn't do it just because I thought I would get a tremendous amount back. It felt really good to have these random checks go out to charities and they would be like, "Wow! Who is this guy?"

Just being able to share the treasure, like you said, at this point.

FRANK: But look at what's happened to your business. It's exploded. There's a reason. There's an absolute design to that success, Yanik. The folks who don't understand that are the ones who are going to wallow in mediocrity for the rest of their lives.

YANIK: The interesting thing is when I decided on that, it didn't start off being big five-figure checks or anything like that. It got easier to write those checks when I said this is the rule for how I run my business.

FRANK: That's great! I want to be able to borrow that at some point. Because Yanik uses the term, "It's the rule," it's part of the business plan. It's not like this is a chore. If you're giving and it's a chore, you shouldn't give. If you're sharing your blessings with those less fortunate and it's a pain in the ass, then you shouldn't be doing it. It is part of Yanik's responsibility to do so. He recognizes it as a responsibility and he embraces it as a responsibility. Look how good he's doing.

YANIK: Right. Actually, I want to clarify one thing. It's 5 percent of the gross, which includes about 10 percent of the net. Just so I don't give people the wrong number and they think, "Yanik is full of BS."

FRANK: Whatever it is, it's tens of thousands of dollars.

YANIK: It ends up pretty good.

Let's move on or we're never going to get to the other secrets.

FRANK: I'm sorry. I get long-winded.

YANIK: No, it's great! I like when you dig deep into it because it gives you a lot of insight.

Let's talk about one of the things in your book that I thought was really insightful. That was, "Why do you want to create a personal value or mission statement." It's something that I haven't done in a formal sense. I would love to hear your comments on it.

FRANK: My first one I did about 12 years ago. I update it annually. I felt and had read in the past—I don't remember where I read this, it was a long while ago—if the United States has a Constitution to govern and guide its citizens, why shouldn't I have a personal constitution?

Why shouldn't I put together a vision statement? It's more than a mission statement; it's a vision statement for my life that when things get a little out of kilter, or are tempted to become out of balance, I can refer to. It takes time. It's not something you can just sit down at your desk and just do. It took me months and months to come up with something that is no longer than a third of a page, including three or four paragraphs—short, little, one- or two-sentence paragraphs.

What is it? What vision is it that you have for your life? I'm a big believer in writing things down and you will see it come to fruition. I would go on a personal retreat. Somewhere very far away from where my nine-to-five existence was. By myself.

I remember one year I went to St. Lucia. One year I went to the Cayman Islands. One year I went to the top of a mountain in Colorado. I really had my own little retreat and began to formulate my personal vision statement.

Once I've got that written down and it's something—where I am right now at this moment is not in front of me. I'm at one of our job sites. In my tree house where my office is, I have it plastered right in front of my face. I look at that thing every single day to make sure I'm on track.

Very few of us are born with an overabundant supply of what I call "vitamin M," which is internally generated motivation. We need to typically get this from outside sources. I generated the mission statement. By looking at it and reading it, it keeps me focused. We're all tempted to go off track. We're all tempted to not live up to the expectation we have for ourselves.

With that personal vision statement and the fact that I keep it current every year, it's been a very invaluable tool for me.

YANIK: Is that beyond just goal setting? Is it beyond finding out what your true value is?

FRANK: Yes, it's way beyond. There's never a checkmark next to the vision statement. It's not a to-do list. It's a guiding principle. Listeners, go take a look at the Constitution. That thing has been around more than a couple of hundred years—230 years. That is the kind of vision that you want to have for your life. It is one that withstands the test of time, something that you can apply today; you can apply ten years from now.

I'm constantly kind of raising the bar with the vision. Getting back to that principle that to whom much is entrusted, much is expected. I tell employees around here if I ever come into work one day and say, "Let's just do it the way we did it on the last house. We did well. We sold the house in six days," you ought to go start looking for a job because I've lost the fire.

The same thing holds true for the vision statement. It's got to be a holistic approach to how you envision living your life both professionally and spiritually, how you want to be perceived, the legacy you want to leave. It's almost like that headstone test. What is my headstone, what is my eulogy going to read looking back?

You've got a chance to dictate what it is that's going to be said at your funeral. It all starts with how much thought you put into that vision statement.

YANIK: Is it pretty broad or is it really specific about things like, "I'm going to be earning x number of dollars?"

FRANK: Let me see if I can find mine on my computer. It is very broad.

YANIK: So it's just guidelines.

FRANK: Yes. It's a guide and a compass.

YANIK: OK. While you're looking for that, I want to talk to you about my favorite thing. I always joke with my wife, Missy, that to be extraordinary, you can't be ordinary. You sum it up in a different way. What was it you said?

FRANK: To live an extraordinary life, you must resist an ordinary approach.

YANIK: OK.

FRANK: Very simple. Going back to the days when I was teaching tennis to very wealthy people—by the way, where I earned my Ph.D. in entrepreneurship and my Masters in real estate was on that tennis court teaching people who walked the talk. This is pre-infomercial, late night "buy my real estate course and learn how to make a million dollars." This was people that had actually done it.

This was probably around the time Carleton Sheets came out. He's been around more than 20 years. These were people I just admired. They drove up to their tennis lesson in a fancy car. They had a beautiful wife and kids and a yacht. I wanted to learn from them. I didn't have the benefit of going to school. This was my classroom out on the tennis court.

What I found was characteristics that—most ordinary people find solace in habits, usually bad ones, and in vices. If you look at the extraordinary people that you look up to—I mean, really look up to. I'm not talking about the flash-in-the-pan. I'm talking about the ones who have been around for a while. They don't oversleep. They don't overeat. They don't drink. They don't take drugs. They don't gamble. They don't womanize.

On and on. There is a whole list of things in my book that I talk about that I started to just get rid of. Those are ordinary—and a lot of them are fine. If you go to Las Vegas and you want to gamble, that's cool. You want to have a glass of wine with dinner, that's fine with me. But when they become a vice and when they become a drain on your highest calling, that's when you've got to look back, take stock, and say, "You know what? My idol, my mentor, doesn't do those things."

People I looked up to back then in the early days, these were people that weren't household names. These were people I just saw living the dream, the *Lifestyle of the Rich and Famous with Robin Leach* days. I just wanted that. I realized that to get it I had to stop doing some things that were damaging to me.

To live the extraordinary life that I'm able to live, the extraordinary life that you're able to live, with your family and your new children and this whole Maverick Business Ventures thing, people are going to come on that because they want a piece of the extraordinary life that it represents.

It's simple. It really is an easy way by process of elimination to live an extraordinary life. You have no business complaining if you go down your black list of the things you do that are unhealthy, unwealthy, and unwise. You have nobody to blame but yourself.

I can sit here and talk until the cows come home. Until you decide to make a lifestyle change, nothing's going to change.

YANIK: The extraordinary part carries over so much than just your own personal habits like what you were talking about, Frank. It goes beyond your houses, the type of Hollywood production you have for the grand openings. I've been invited to a recent one. Unfortunately, I couldn't make it. I've seen videos of you jumping the motorcycle over the house—not over, but in front of the house.

FRANK: It actually was over.

YANIK: It was over the house?

FRANK: It was over.

YANIK: [Laughing] So if you missed, you land through the roof.

FRANK: Actually, I jumped a motorcycle over the replica of my very first house I did. It was a very small house.

YANIK: [Laughing] All right.

FRANK: Not the mega house. No, no.

YANIK: [Laughing] I see that carrying over in everything that you do. That's the way I think about it, too. If somebody is doing something one way, why do it that same way? Why not put your unique stamp on it, be extraordinary.

I guess that kind of carries over to another part of your secrets, which is having the flair in everything that you do.

FRANK: I think the important lesson there is I have competitors in my industry that I'm actually very good friends with. One of them is Mark Pulte from the Pulte Home family. He doesn't use his last name; he uses Mark Timothy which is his middle name.

He deviated from the family business and he builds beautiful mega-mansions on spec. We go to lunch regularly. He's the polar opposite of me; he's very conservative with a nice banker's haircut, very soft-spoken, doesn't really do grand unveilings; if he does, it's a three-piece quartet with a harpist.

Yet he does very well, so what he does and the niche he's carved out works extremely well for him. He's branded himself.

Taking a contrarian approach to life is more often than not very rewarding. It can be financially rewarding. When I say contrarian approach it's really, using a real estate term, location, location, location.

I don't buy it; I don't follow it; I never have followed it; I've gone the opposite; I've made markets where they hadn't existed before. That's a business model, and you can look at Michael Dell or Bill Gates or anybody whom you look up to who established a marketplace. They went in an opposite direction from the herd. That is living an extraordinary life.

Life is actually, as you and I have in common, about experiences; it's not about sitting back and reading about somebody else's experiences. I like to create what I call my own reality. I know that sounds a little far out there.

I watch a little bit of the news, which I hate, but I have to keep current, especially on the financial side. But there's a reason, Yanik, that I work out of a tree house. You'll get to see that when you come down in November. I have a beautiful ocean-front tree house with 12 windows in it. I've got a shower; I've got a toilet; I've got a sink; I've got broadband; I've got a bamboo desk, hardwood floors; I've got a loft with a king-size bed and a flat screen TV. It's my domain.

Now I have a main office where everybody else works. I go there once a month. I'm not an architect, but I create this 70,000-square-foot house with 22 bedrooms, 24 bathrooms, and an 18-car garage. I created that up there. I wrote my books up there.

I'm a firm believer in creating one's own reality via life's experiences. I've gone on your website and you like getting up in front of people and doing a comedy routine. That was hilarious! That took a lot of guts and built a lot of confidence in you. I'm sure I couldn't do something like that.

YANIK: The funny thing is I was actually more nervous to do that than stand in front of 3,000 people that I spoke to in the UK last year.

FRANK: I'm sure, because if you bomb, the tomatoes don't feel too good.

YANIK: Yeah. Where is that confidence? Where is that kind of "gumption," for lack of a better word, that you said that you can design your own reality?

FRANK: It starts very simply. It starts with celebrating each little, humble victory in your life as a triumph and achievement. That's a long way of saying "building confidence."

Celebrate each humble victory. When we were kids, assuming you had a decent set of parents or even relatives, you were patted on the back or on the head quite often. "Great job, Yanik! You brought home an A today. Great job, Yanik! You built a fire in Boy Scouts!"

Whatever it is, we got the pat on the back. But that went away when we left home and often people are very busy trying to tear us down, especially those who succeed at a higher level, trying to find fault, shoot holes through your theories and concepts, and what have you.

Well, I learned at an early age that I needed to celebrate each humble victory as a triumph and achievement, which, in turn, caused me to build confidence, and in building confidence I was able to say "yes" to opportunities more than "no," therefore, the experiences I was able to create for myself, the reality of not being influenced.

This is true especially now. I know this call isn't about real estate, but I'll tell you what. You don't have to be in real estate to realize the negativity and the pundits that are just slamming the real estate markets right now.

I'm going around the country doing this 911 emergency, "Frank, please come and talk to my real estate investment club, because my members are freaking out with all the negativity that's permeating the airwaves."

I don't buy it. There are factual issues about the real estate market. I'm calling it The Great Real Estate Depression of '07. "Frank! You're Mr. Glass Is Half Full. How can you say those words?" It is a reality. We've never seen a market like this since 1929.

Where do the opportunities lie? Where's the silver lining? We're not going to get into that; I'll save that for another call, but they're there and I'm going to show you how to find them. That's because I live by my own reality. I live with this abundance mentality, knowing that I can create my own profits when everybody else is being in despair.

YANIK: Right there. That's another great insight into your character, not letting external forces dictate where you think the profits are going to be.

FRANK: Never. Don't get me wrong; I do my homework. I'm not a seat-of-the-pants kind of guy. Some of the best deals I've made in my life, Yanik, are the deals I didn't make. I know when not to pursue something.

At the same time, when the talking heads are on CNBC, I'm usually the only one, like on Fox recently, where I took the opposite side of the argument. Yeah, real estate values are down across the country for the first time since 1929, and yeah, foreclosure rates in Florida have doubled over the past year; even across the country they've gone up 36 percent month over month.

I can quote all the stats, but what are you going to do about it? Are you going to sit there and complain as the talking head does or, if you're a real estate investor, wouldn't you imagine this is the best time since 1929 to be out there in the real estate marketplace buying? It is!

It's like if you could call a bottom in Microsoft or Dell or Intel or what have you, you call bottom on that stock and you knew what the bottom was, wouldn't you buy it? You would because those are strong stocks.

The same thing holds true for the commodity known as real estate.

YANIK: Excellent. Going back to your time as a tennis instructor and learning from successful people and now firsthand dealing with them, the people that buy your houses, talk about some of the things you've learned and what makes truly successful people tick and why you should learn from them.

FRANK: I think we covered that when we said, "To live an extraordinary life you must resist an ordinary approach." Mind you, I've sold 36,000 since 1992 and I know that doesn't sound like a lot, but each one of them averaged 12 million bucks.

I haven't sold one to anybody who has inherited money. I've sold every house to people who have earned it by being a titan of their own industry in some way, shape, or form. I've found that they're extremely disciplined, which doesn't come naturally. I am now very disciplined, in bed at 9:00, up at 4:30 every day, except Sundays I get up at 6:00.

They are extremely quick decision-makers. I've witnessed it! They walk in the door of my house on a Tuesday, and we're talking about a $12 million purchase, and they're sleeping there on Friday night.

I can't make that big of a decision that quickly! Most of us can't decide on what pair of shoes to buy in the mall. But what I've learned is that psychologically what we do, and I say "we" as the average person, that's detrimental as compared to the ultra wealthy when it comes time to make a decision, is think we need to do an exorbitant amount of research. With the information that's available to us today, to do such research, we've got to dig deeper into spreadsheets, and we've got to do a comparative market analysis, and so on.

What we're doing, Yanik, is making excuses to pull the freakin' trigger. These guys—not just in buying my houses, that's the way they live their life—they gather the data very quickly and then they use their initial intuition is what typically tips the scales in which direction to make the decision.

Many people say, "You know what? This house isn't for me. I'm not going to do it." When it comes time for me to see an opportunity, you better believe that the old paralysis by analysis does no longer set in with Frank McKinney because I've watched the wealthy make very rapid-fire decisions, huge decisions that you and I and the average person would see as almost irresponsible.

But you know what? They're not irresponsible. But they're not looking for a way, subliminally and subconsciously, like the rest of us are, to actually say, "Ah! Well, this one item on the spreadsheet tells me I shouldn't do it! I finally found the reason why I shouldn't pursue this new internet business!" If you look hard enough, you'll find a reason not to do it.

YANIK: That's a great point. I like that. If you look hard enough you always find a reason not to do something.

But also, you're not advocating, like you said before, seat-of-your-pants and just completely winging it.

FRANK: No, but I am advocating that if you're unsure, go back to that seat-of-the-pants intuition that you had at the very onset of your research to allow you to kind of tip the scales.

YANIK: Talk about your intuition. I'm always fascinated by that in successful people. How do you use that? Have you seen that used? Do people really make big decisions that way?

FRANK: Yes. They do, and intuition is something that, fortunately, we're all born with. It's something that needs to be exercised; it's something that needs to be visited very, very often.

The unfortunate thing is that most of us doubt ours. We doubt it; we kill it; we squash it like a bug. We don't allow our subconscious to act on that intuition. Let it happen! Let it flow! Go with it and see what happens!

This is an easy post-mortem, but how many times can you go back in your life and say, "Boy, I wish I would have. I was right the first time, darn it!"

I do a lot of the post-mortems. I look back; when we're done with a project we get together. I shouldn't say "post-mortem"; that's kind of negative. But after the whole thing's over, we review what we did right and wrong, and often the things we did wrong were because we pondered too long; we contemplated too long, instead of just running with it.

YANIK: How do you open up more of that intuition, or how do you make sure that you're listening to it?

FRANK: Well, the first thing you do is carve your niche a little deeper and a little wider than most, but you stick within your niche.

In the real estate circles now, what's unfortunate is that you have so many different ways to make money in real estate. You have being a contractor, being a renovator, being a flipper, or being a buy and hold. You have commercial real estate; you have short sales; you have wholesaling. I could go on and on.

The unfortunate thing is that very few people spend enough time carving that niche a little deeper and a little wider. The whole reason I wrote my second book, Yanik, is because I take the reader on this journey from a $50,000 fixer-upper to a $100,000,000 mansion. I know people who can talk the concept, but I don't know anybody who can walk the talk.

I have done that! I'm in the same niche! I haven't deviated in the least! I'm still doing what I was doing 21 years ago, only there are a bunch more zeros at the end of the acquisition and sale price.

By sticking with that niche I now know, my intuition is so keen when it comes to knowing what to do in order to touch the five senses, sight, sound, smell, touch, and taste, of my buyers and raising the experience that my buyers have with their five senses to the state of subliminal euphoria, I mean drunkenness, to where they can act on their own intuition and buy my property, rapid fire.

The important lesson there is to stick within the niche. You hone your skill. I know within half an hour when somebody walks through the door of one of my houses if they're qualified and if they're going to buy it. It's because I've spent 21 years honing the intuition specifically to the field of my expertise.

YANIK: That's interesting. I guess the more and more you listen to your intuition, the stronger it gets and the more you can rely on it.

FRANK: That's a good point. Listening to it is one thing, but acting on it is another. We first have to listen and recognize that typically, more often than not, our initial intuition is going to be right. With pulling the trigger and acting on it, we're going to be right and then we're going to be right again, and then, oops, we're going to be wrong once.

That seems to set most people back to ground zero, and that's unfortunate. I don't look at it that way. Sometimes I have pulled the trigger, relied on my intuition, and been wrong. As you know, we learn more from our mistakes than from our successes, so I get into what it was that

I did wrong and where did I take the left when I should have taken the right, and I make sure it doesn't happen again.

YANIK: Excellent. Let's talk about something that you have, obviously, become very good at and that's what you call gently, yet progressively, flexing your risk muscle and threshold.

FRANK: In Chapter 25, my second favorite chapter in my first book, it says, "Gently, yet often, exercise your risk threshold, which is your risk tolerance, your tolerance for risk, like a muscle. Eventually it will become stronger and able to withstand greater pressure."

If I was looking out over the same group of 3,000 real-estate wannabes, and I was giving a talk and trying to inspire them to get involved in the business to make a bunch of money in real estate, what I've quantified over the last, probably, decade is that the difference between me and most who are pursuing a professional career in real estate investing is my ability to exercise that risk threshold.

It doesn't matter if you're going to be the president of the neighborhood Tupperware club, or if you're going to start an internet business, or if you're going to get into the real estate business, we have to be able to embrace fear and risk. It doesn't mean we're not afraid; Frank McKinney is afraid every single day of his life, but I've never let that fear stop me. That's the big difference.

"Oh, Frank, you're a daredevil. You have disregard for your body and your financial well-being." That's a bunch of crap. I will tell you one thing. I'm a lot less exciting than I look. My wife calls me a nerd in sheep's clothing based upon the research that I do and the fact that when it's time to exercise that risk threshold, I do it.

Mind you, I've done it for 21 years. I know no other way, Yanik. I get paid once or twice a year, contrary to a lot of multiple streams of income. That's not my niche; I don't do it. I wait to get paid when I sell a big house. We have some other investments that actually do pay a little bit every month.

But if you take nothing else from this call today, go to Chapter 25. If you buy the book, go right there, make a beeline for that chapter and read how important it is. Regardless of whether you're listening because your husband or wife made you listen to this call, it's about embracing risk and embracing fear, staring it in the eyes, recognizing it for what it is, and not letting it stop you.

How many folks are listening who have what I call the nine-to-five cubicle mentality? By the way, none of us are born internet business builders and none of us are born real estate investors; we're all doing something else before we get to this real estate business or internet business. What is it going to take to get you out from behind your nine-to-five cubicle?

When we're done here, go to www.Frank-McKinney.com and click on "About Frank McKinney." Underneath that is "Frank's Top 10 Reading List." Click that and you'll see about 20 books, even though I still call it the Top 10. One of my favorite books is written by one of my favorite philosophers, Anthony DeMello. He looks at fear this way. He says, "We've been conditioned since adolescence to fear the unknown."

Fear of the unknown, right? You've heard it, Yanik, right?

YANIK: Right.

FRANK: Fear of the unknown; I've heard it. He dispels that notion in a very clear way in that he says, "How is it possible that we fear something we are unaware of? How is it possible to fear something we don't know?"

It's not possible! What's possible and what happens is that we fear leaving the known. We don't fear the unknown because we can't! It's unknown! We fear leaving the known.

We fear leaving the nine-to-five cubicle mentality; we fear leaving the tennis court, in my case. When I was a tennis pro, I was dreadfully fearful of putting my hard-earned money into that first $50,000 fixer-upper.

So exercising that risk threshold like a muscle very early on and in small increments like going to the gym and starting to do curls with a two-pound dumbbell and moving up to a 40-pound dumbbell, that's what it's like. After a period of time you'll get there and you'll then realize when you're confronted with fear, it's usually associated with opportunity.

What's your choice? I mean, fear, risk, or don't risk. If you don't risk you're just going to maintain that cubicle mentality. You risk it, and I'm not talking about gambling. Frank McKinney will walk through a casino to get ideas but I'll never put a quarter in a slot machine. There's a big difference between calculated risk and gambling.

Where do you think your life is going to lead if you can exercise that risk threshold like a muscle?

YANIK: So you suggest progressively moving that forward, not just taking one big leap?

FRANK: No. That's the beauty of [*Frank McKinney's Maverick Approach to Real Estate Success: How You can Go From a $50,000 Fixer Upper to a $100 Million Mansion*]. Even if you're not into real estate, I take you on this journey that starts with a $50,000 fixer-upper. I offer up today that the biggest risk I ever took was that first $50,000 fixer-upper, pulling that trigger, taking my hard-earned money. This was before other people's money. I earned $36,000 baking out there in the hot sun, teaching tennis, and I took that and bought that first property. That was the most significant risk I ever took in my life.

YANIK: Excellent. All right, let's talk about the simple thing you can do each day to make sure you're having fun and following your journey. You said that your wife says here that you're what?

FRANK: I'm a nerd in sheep's clothing.

YANIK: You definitely have a lot of fun, regardless. It might not be every single day that you're out there living it up and jumping motorcycles or doing the crazy things that you do like running 135 miles in the hundred-gazillion-degree heat.

But what do you do each day to make sure that you're having fun?

FRANK: The best lesson I could give on that is, again, from my first book. I know some of you don't need me to teach you because I know you live it.

In Chapter 46 it says, "Each day, you're on the concert stage of life, so you better make it rock. Approach each day with a little flair."

I'll never forget going to see Siegfried and Roy for the first time before he had his accident. We were sitting in the audience and they were great performers. There was a couple that was celebrating their 15th wedding anniversary and they had seen Siegfried and Roy on their honeymoon 15 years before.

I was overhearing them talk about the energy that the show had and that it was even better than they remembered 15 years before and how the performers gave their all.

If you're into rock 'n' roll groups, KISS is another example. They've been around for a long time and they give it their best every day on the concert stage of life, so you'd better make it rock.

We don't need to be performers, but aren't we a performer in our own right with regard to what we do for a living? So for me, I wake up every day, and like you said, every day it's not jumping motorcycles over houses. A lot of days I'm on a construction site wearing construction boots with a hard hat on, eating my lunch with the rest of the workers out there.

But I want to make sure that by the end of the day I have made an impact on the legacy that I am ultimately going to leave behind when I'm gone. A lot of that has to do with the nonprofit stuff that we do. I'm working towards that next 135-mile race across the desert or whatever it may be, or the next theatrical presentation when it comes time for the unveiling of one of our masterpieces. That makes life worth living.

I've always felt that 97 percent of our life is spent in ordinary times pursuing the extraordinarily gold moments as represented by 3 percent. Really, when you think about it, we're all in pursuit mode and we're pursuing something. We're in ordinary time, and then we get married. Remember when you had your children, Yanik, how extraordinarily golden that was; when you made your first million; when we sold our first house. There are not a lot of times, so I just try to recognize and embrace that 97 percent as I'm going through it and try to bring a little flair to those multiple minutes.

11 X-FACTORS TO LIVE BY

THE MAVERICK STARTUP STRATEGY

X-Factor 1: Creating the Big Idea or "Hook"

X-Factor 2: Your Vision

X-Factor 3: High Margins and Premium Prices

X-Factor 4: Get it Out the Door NOW!

X-Factor 5: Test and Improve

X-Factor 6: Listen and Shift

X-Factor 7: Create Zealots

X-Factor 8: What's Next?

X-Factor 9: Tap Your MasterMind

X-Factor 10: Create the Fun

X-Factor 11: Create the Impact

These maverick rules are the "little hinges" that swing big doors of opportunity to fast-track your idea. Put these to work creating a breakthrough for your product, creating super fans, building buzz, and making an impact all while doing well. This is a golden era for entrepreneurship with small bets turning into big-time successes. I can't wait to hear your story!

ABOUT THE AUTHOR

Yanik Silver is a serial entrepreneur who has built multiple successful online businesses, even though he still considers himself a "techno dunce." He has successfully bootstrapped eight different product and service ideas, hitting the million-dollar sales mark from scratch, without funding, taking on debt, or even having a real business plan. Yanik's story and businesses have been featured in *Business 2.0*, *Fox Business News*, TIME.com, *USA Today*, SmartMoney. com, *The Wall Street Journal*, *MSN Money*, Conde Naste's Portfolio. com, Entrepreneur.com, *WIRED* magazine, WORTH.com, *The Boston Globe*, *Denver Business Journal*, and many others.

He is the author of several bestselling marketing books and tools, including *Moonlighting on the Internet*, *Instant Sales Letters®*, and *34 Rules for Maverick Entrepreneurs*. Yanik is also the founder of the Underground® Online Seminar and Maverick1000, a private group of game-changing entrepreneurs.

As a self-described "adventure junkie," Yanik has found that his own life-changing experiences such as running with the bulls, bungee jumping, HALO skydiving, exotic car rallies, and Zero-Gravity flights have not only expanded his limits but also led to breakthroughs in ideas, focus, and business thinking. In between checking off items on his Ultimate Big Life List, he calls Potomac, Maryland, home with his wife, Missy, and two mini maverick adventurers in the making, Zack and Zoe.

You Can Continue to Connect with Yanik

Yanik's Blogs

www.MaverickMBA.com and www.InternetLifestyle.com

On Twitter

www.Twitter.com/yaniksilver

Additional Resources from Yanik Silver

www.InstantSalesLetters.com

www.UndergroundOnlineSeminar.com

www.Maverick1000.com

www.MaverickBusinessAdventures.com

Additional Resource for Maverick Startups:

InstantSalesLetters®

Stop Writing Sales Letters The Hard Way! Here's How To Turn Any Company Into A Booming Business…

In Only 2½ Minutes You Can Quickly and Easily Create A Sales Letter Guaranteed To Sell Your Product Or Service…
Without Writing!

Looking To Increase Your Business?
Just Fill In A Few Blanks And PRESTO…
You've Just Created A Powerful, Money-Making Sales Letter!

Imagine…one letter (or email) could bring you tons of hot leads and new customers, get them to keep buying over and over again, reactivate 'lost' customers, and even provide you with a constant stream of referrals. So anytime you need more business - you simply turn the tap on… it's like having the goose that lays the golden egg.

Nearly Every Sales Piece You Need Is Already Written For You…

Over 25,000 different business owners and entrepreneurs have successfully used the original Instant Sales Letters® based on proven marketing principles and psychology. But now we've completely updated them and made it better than ever with new online web templates, emails and extra bonuses.

No Matter What Product or Service You Have To Sell - You'll Find A Sales Letter, Email or Web Template That's Already Written For You…

⚙ **BUSINESS TO BUSINESS** LETTERS   💼 **PROFESSIONAL** LETTERS

💡 **INFORMATION PRODUCT** LETTERS

🗑 **RETAIL** LETTERS   🎁 **SERVICE** LETTERS   🌐 **BUSINESS OPPORTUNITY & NETWORK MARKETING** LETTERS

www.InstantSalesLetters.com

INDEX